Conscious Collaboration

Ben Emmens

Conscious Collaboration

Re-Thinking The Way We Work Together, For Good

palgrave
macmillan

Ben Emmens
The Conscious Project
United Kingdom

ISBN 978-1-137-53803-1   ISBN 978-1-137-53805-5   (eBook)
DOI 10.1057/978-1-137-53805-5

Library of Congress Control Number: 2016943403

This Palgrave Macmillan imprint is published by Springer Nature
The registered company is Macmillan Publishers Ltd. London

To Abi, my thinking partner and conscious collaborator.
In memory of my father, Stuart, whose collaborative spirit burns brightly.

Foreword

Almost every challenge we face in our communities, regions and countries can only be solved when people choose to collaborate with each other. Collaboration is a relatively easy principle for most people—indeed the success of our species has in part been because we are able and willing to collaborate and share with others. We naturally collaborate with people whom we know, and preferably with people in our kinship group, with people whom we have a great deal in common, and with people whom we see and relate to often.

The real collaborative challenge is not this natural form of collaboration. It is about solving challenges by collaborating with people who are very different from us, people whom we may not know, and indeed with people whom we rarely if ever see.

That is complex, conscious collaboration, and it requires a great deal of skill, competence and know-how. More often than not this type of collaboration also requires the involvement of more than one party. Indeed, it is the success of these multi-stakeholder collaborations that will determine whether the big challenges we face right now can be solved.

Over the last decade there has been a growing awareness of this type of collaboration and a growing expertise in how to navigate the many challenges it creates. That is why "conscious collaboration" is so crucial. Conscious in the sense that complex collaboration rarely succeeds without the conscious application of skills, competencies and know-how; and conscious in the sense that some of the very best examples of collaboration are driven by a sense of purpose. When each party is striving towards a purpose that is greater than their individual needs, there is an opportunity for enormous energy and goodwill to be unleashed.

It is relatively easy to describe the theory of complex collaboration. What is a great deal more difficult, but potentially also a great deal more rewarding, is to build insights from the act of collaboration. This is what Ben Emmens has done. Through many years of actively pushing the boundaries of collaboration, of bringing in multiple stakeholders and of working as a collaborative leader he is sharing with us his insights and wisdom. During this period of experimentation and learning he has pushed his own boundaries, worked at the edges of the systems that he inhabits and developed ways of thinking about how commitments are made, how accountabilities described and how processes evolve over time.

In a sense Ben picks up where I left off with my book on collaboration, *Hot Spots*. When writing that book we had begun to be aware that collaborating, particularly complex collaboration, was a conscious process. It was clear to me that creating a culture of collaboration, building collaborative networks and working towards an igniting purpose were the three most crucial stages. What Ben has done is to live collaboration consciously in his daily work and in doing so has brought insights and actionable wisdom that go far beyond my own theoretical underpinning. He has created ideas about collaboration that will take the conversation a great deal forward.

Lynda Gratton
Professor of Management Practice,
London Business School,
London, UK

Preface

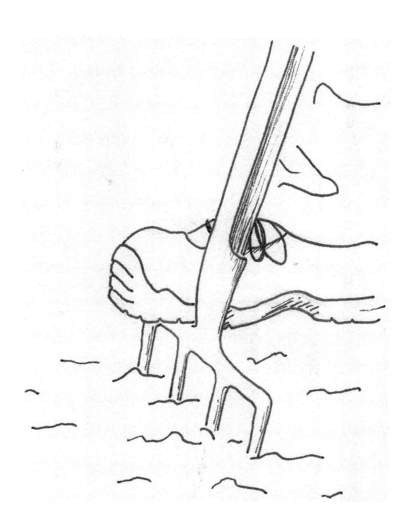

As I look around at what feels like an increasingly individualized and selfish world, I'm convinced we need to live and work more consciously, and this book is about me exploring and expressing what that might look like. Conversations and reflections with colleagues, friends and family during the thinking and writing process have only served to heighten my growing sense of awareness that, collectively, we need to rethink how we work together.

My first practical experience of what I would call collaboration was back in the mid-1980s. Growing up as a teenager in a rural farming community in the south-west of England, it seemed that survival—and ultimately success—was dependent on knowing useful people and being a useful person to know. I recognize our family was not the only one that relied on an informal bartering system for goods and services: we've got a mower, you've got a tractor and a plow, he's got a trailer, she is a vet, you're good at bookkeeping, they've got chickens, we've got sheep, the neighbor's an electrician, we have a market garden, and so forth. My memory is of a sort of symbiotic community where folk generally helped one another to achieve what was needed, knowing that there would soon be a time when they themselves would need help.

The second profound experience came later. In my early twenties, I saw collaboration scaled across a much larger geographic area and with a diverse set of individuals, as my parents mobilized an extraordinary team of 'unusual suspects' to provide event support and sports timing services for mountain bike races all over the UK. The early 1990s were formative years for the sport of mountain biking and most definitely uncharted territory for the British Cycling Federation, which at the time was struggling to keep up with growing interest in a new sport which was ill-equipped to run national events by itself.

Both those experiences made me realize that some of the best collaborations grow when there is a real need and individuals have a real desire to step in and address that need. The latter example also made me understand that collaboration can thrive in uncharted territory, where the lack of any real precedence in terms of approach gives individuals the freedom to be creative. I learned a lot about co-operation in the 1990s, both through the experience of my parents in their work and also myself as I graduated and entered the world of work. My enduring memory of my parents' collaborative venture at that time was that it was an exhilarating and simultaneously exhausting adventure, fraught with risk (of failure or mistakes), yet somehow utterly compelling. The elation shared when a national event was a success carried them on to the next challenge. Looking back, I can clearly see my father's role in the collaborative endeavor—a unique leader in the local community, able to pull together a range of organizations and unite them around a shared vision. It takes courage and audacity to boldly articulate a vision that compels others to rally round, and somehow—by being in the right place at the right time, seeing the need, and having a good idea of the skills and competencies required to address the need—he was able to mobilize a diverse team, broker a deal to provide the services and see it through to success. My father was always able to get people to work together—he'd cut his teeth running local youth clubs, which certainly required patience and the ability to act as a peacemaker. He also had a small ego, which meant he was happiest when in service to a great cause and when playing a part in bringing about a great outcome.

These two very personal experiences of collaboration were undoubtedly formative for me. However, if we look back at history we see scattered examples of collaboration that changed the world. They may have been less well-known collaborations in ancient times, when rulers and tribes often came together for reasons of politics and power—or well-known examples from the twenty-first century, such as Apple, Google, Facebook and Microsoft, all of them changed the way we live and work. It's interesting to me that each of those twenty-first-century organizations began as a collaborative endeavor between two or three individuals, often in a garage or small office, and what sets these collaborations apart, for me, is the fact that they were what I would call conscious: individuals chose to collaborate to create something new, and the collaboration was born out of a combination of idealistic vision, child-like curiosity, stubborn perseverance and sheer tenacity. The individuals were open to all sorts of possibilities. It's unusual for a great collaboration to begin with a surfeit of cash or resources—they typically require inventiveness, resourcefulness and creativity to overcome a range of obstacles—including not having much money. In fact, as we will see, money often complicates collaboration.

I've often wondered where collaboration comes from and what drives it. Does it come from the head, the heart, or the head *and* the heart? What else is required? If I want to collaborate with someone do I need to find a kindred spirit or am I just as likely to find success with someone I merely get along with most of the time? It certainly appears to be the case that collaboration succeeds when there is a conscious engagement by those collaborating, when there is a practical outcome that gives satisfaction and when the experience is stimulating and emotionally or spiritually satisfying. Drawing on the examples above it's clear, therefore, that conscious collaboration is about timing, leadership, vision, stubbornness, commitment, learning, outcomes and an active engagement of head and heart. These are some of the things I hope to explore in this book as I set out the case for rethinking how we work together.

Writing a book is quite an undertaking and I must thank three people in particular for inspiring me to put my thinking down on paper. The first is my father, Stuart, whom I have already mentioned; his humility in leadership and tireless commitment to working with others for good inspired so many, but was cut short by his tragic death in 1996. The second is my wife and co-director at The Conscious Project, Abi Green; her vision, pragmatism energy and constant desire to make this world a better place amazes and inspires me. And the third person is one of the most brilliant organizational thinkers of our time, Lynda Gratton; it's been a privilege to work with Lynda as part of her Future of Work Research Consortium and her thinking on collaboration and early encouragement to write my own thoughts down sowed a seed which grew into this book.

I hope that this book sparks some thinking and catalyzes reflection for you individually and for those you work with. Collaboration is a journey of discovery and there's more to be written and shared. Come and join the debate at consciouscollaboration.org.

Ben Emmens
London, UK

Acknowledgments

Just as it 'takes a village to raise a child', it takes many people to bring a book into being. I am indebted to all those who have shared insights, wisdom and encouragement along the way, and to those who have practically supported this book through contributing examples and their practical experience. Particular thanks are due to the indomitable Mike Johnson who catalyzed the opportunity for me to write my thinking down. Mike is the Chairman of the Future Work Forum, a global think-tank whose focus is the future of work. I'm proud to be counted as a partner of the Future Work Forum, and to have Mike as a friend and confidant. And special thanks are also due to Stephen Partridge at Palgrave Macmillan for the opportunity to publish and to Abi Green, my co-director and thinking partner at The Conscious Project, for her patience, understanding, encouragement and super illustrations.

I'd also like to acknowledge the following for their inspiration and encouragement along the way: Lynda Gratton at the Hot Spots Movement, for her inspiration and drive and for encouraging me to write; Jonathan Potter, formerly Executive Director at People In Aid, for giving me space to learn, lead and collaborate; Kate Nowlan, CEO of CiC Employee Assistance, for being a thinking partner and a voice of reason; Paul Knox Clarke at ALNAP, for pioneering research into leadership and collaboration in the aid sector; David and Clare Hieatt, co-founders of the Do Lectures and Hiut Denim for inspiring us to launch

The Conscious Project and reminding me that ideas create change; John V. Willshire at Smithery, for his energy, creativity, ideas and the genius Artefact cards; Sara Swords at Sara Swords Coaching, for her patience, support, encouragement and vision, and the shared collaborative experiences; Sean Lowrie at the Start Network, for his vision and determination to transform the aid sector; Caroline Hotham at the Start Network, for believing in collaboration and giving us space and opportunity to jam; David Hockaday, formerly in the Emergency Capacity Building Project and currently at the Start Network, for his reflective thinking and encouragement; Katy Murray at Katy Catalyst, for her infectious enthusiasm, for being a thinking partner and a critical friend; Ian Gee at Edgelands Consultancy, for his wisdom and thinking on networks, communities and the virtual guild; Lisa McKay at Lisa McKay Writing, for her support, encouragement and conscious collaboration; Ted Lankester at Community Health Global Network, for his generosity, collaborative vision encouragement and for being a great mentor; Rajan Rasaiah at Verve and Values, for the generous hours spent coaching me, and for his friendship and gentle challenge; Liz Emmens, for her encouragement, and belief in the fundamental importance of conscious collaboration.

And to the many others who have encouraged me and shared their ideas and thinking along the way, including: Euan Semple, Betel Tassew, Ed Griffin, Rhian Cadvan-Jones, Alex Swarbrick, Di Willis, Andy Delin, Cath Russ, Tony Moore, Margaret Green, Maurice Green, Ros Tennyson and Gunther Pratz, I offer my sincere thanks. If I've missed you, then please accept my apologies.

Contents

About the Author

Ben Emmens has worked in the aid sector for the last 15 years, holding a range of roles that have seen him work with humanitarian and development agencies in more 40 countries. He spent ten years with People In Aid, an umbrella organization that provided HR and people-management support to those working to reduce inequality and alleviate suffering. Prior to his career in the aid sector, he held a variety of roles in the private and public sectors.

He is the co-founder of The Conscious Project, a social business that typically works at Board, Executive or senior management level and whose client list includes UNICEF, the Red Cross, Action Aid, Save the Children, Oxfam, CARE, World Vision, the International Rescue Committee, the International Water Management Institute, International Food Policy Research Institute, the Scout Association, Amnesty International, the Pakistan Humanitarian Forum and the National Health Service.

List of Figures

1

Introduction

Collaboration, Noun, Verb: Definition

The idea that everyone can work together and produce something better than they could on their own, with less work.

I've often wondered why collaborating so often fails to live up to the initial hype and expectation, leaving the debris of unfulfilled promises and the bitter taste of disappointment and regret at what might have been.

Instead of being more than the sum of its parts, collaboration can often fall victim to self-interest, lack of focus, an evaporating vision, an aversion to risk and sometimes outright dissent. Some collaborations wither away or die a slow and painful death, others are killed or abruptly

© The Editor(s) (if applicable) and The Author(s) 2016
B. Emmens, *Conscious Collaboration*,
DOI 10.1057/978-1-137-53805-5_1

curtailed, and others still are, to borrow a veterinary term, put down humanely. All of these have been true for various collaborations I've been involved with over the last 20 years, and I've read countless stories where other collaborations have met the same fate.

The failure of collaboration is especially poignant given the nature and complexity of the challenges our society faces today. Some of the social and environmental problems we encounter seem intractable, or at least of a scale such that no single entity is equipped or able to solve them, least of all the United Nations, or political and economic entities such as the European Union.

Our interconnected and interdependent world and the sheer scale of the challenges we face requires us to transform the way we collaborate. Challenges such as climate change, urbanization, the mass displacement of communities and families, youth unemployment, public health emergencies and rising inequality require unprecedented responses from a huge number of different stakeholders. We need to go beyond co-operation—though for sure that would be a great start in many situations I can think of right now—and rethink the way we work together. One of the reasons Abi and I established The Conscious Project in 2012 was in response to what we considered to be the complete unsustainability of many management practices and organizational behaviors. We strongly believed that we needed to rethink how we manage and lead our organizations and particularly our collaborative endeavors, and we were convinced a more conscious approach was required by businesses and nonprofit institutions especially. And—when it comes to collaboration itself—we are absolutely convinced that it has to be *conscious* in order to have a hope of success. But what do we mean by 'conscious collaboration'? The following chapters will shine some light on this and offer some insights which I hope will be useful, as well as challenging.

What Is Collaboration?

Looking up the definition of collaboration is an interesting exercise—and reveals the truth that collaboration isn't always seen as something positive.

For some, collaboration is the idea that everyone can work together to produce something better than they could on their own—with *less work*. However, we know, often from personal experience, that collaboration requires intentionality and considerable investment of time and resources, and it can often result in more work for a few members of the group who drive the collaborative endeavor.

As Jesse Lyn Stoner says, at its simplest, 'collaboration is working together to create something new in support of a shared vision'.[1] The key points are that: it is not through individual effort, something new is created, and that the glue is the shared vision.[2] Although collaboration may arise spontaneously, intuitively we know that successful and sustained collaboration requires commitment and effort. We also know that some of the most successful collaborations have been begun by a group of unusual suspects, not kindred spirits.

Stoner also helpfully distinguishes co-ordination and co-operation from collaboration—all of which are important aspects of teamwork but by no means the same thing. Co-ordination is sharing information and resources so that each party can accomplish their part in support of a mutual objective. It is about teamwork in implementation, and not creating something new together. Co-operation is important in networks where individuals exchange relevant information and resources in support of each other's goals, rather than a shared goal. Something new may be achieved as a result, but it arises from the individual, not from a collective team effort.[3]

Dion Hinchcliffe would appear to have a similar view and helpfully summarizes as follows[4]:

Co-ordination: Let's achieve a common activity
Co-operation: Let's improve something
Collaboration: Let's create something new

---

[1] Jesse Lyn Stoner, Seapoint Center for Collaborative Leadership, http://seapointcenter.com/co-operation-teamwork-and-collaboration/ (accessed September 30, 2015).
[2] Ibid.
[3] Ibid.
[4] http://www.dionhinchcliffe.com (accessed October 1, 2015).

There are many organizations—professional associations and networks, academic institutions and consulting firms in particular—that are currently working to understand and define collaboration. In the aid sector one such organization is ALNAP—the Active Learning Network for Accountability and Performance in Humanitarian Action—which has in recent years invested considerably in the area of work that comes under the heading 'Humanitarian leadership and coordination'.[5] Co-ordination is an important aspect of humanitarian response and shortcomings in this area are repeatedly identified through evaluations and research. In their own research ALNAP have invested time in exploring models of leadership that include aspects of co-operation and collaboration and offer a number of useful ideas to stimulate thinking and guide organization development practitioners. For example, in their recently published report 'Exploring coordination in humanitarian clusters'[6] they found that humanitarian organizations often used the term 'collaboration' to describe a 'more explicit, formalised relationship, in which organizations shared agreed objectives and priorities, and coordinated on multiple things at once',[7] although they suggest that 'alignment' might describe the nature of some collaborative relationships more accurately.[8]

Collaboration, then, is 'a way for aligned organizations to create something new', and in general it is seen as a positive thing.

Describing the Way We Work Together

At this point it's helpful to briefly introduce a simple model that helps us identify 'where an organization is at' when it comes to collaboration. I offer the model below as a basic taxonomy that classifies the various ways we work together; the model and the characteristics of each 'state' are described in more detail in Chap. 15.

---

[5] http://www.alnap.org/what-we-do/leadership-coordination (accessed October 1, 2015).

[6] Exploring coordination in humanitarian clusters, Paul Knox-Clarke and Leah Campbell, ALNAP Study, London, 2015, http://www.alnap.org/resource/20360 (accessed October 1, 2015).

[7] Ibid., p. 7 (accessed October 1, 2015).

[8] Ibid., p. 56 (accessed October 1, 2015).

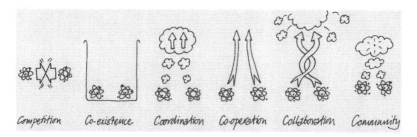

Fig. 1.1 The collaboration continuum

The way we work together, or the 'collaboration continuum'

I've called it the collaboration continuum because although the states or types of relationship are discrete when taken in isolation, when we look at the various ways in which we work together and the ways we can describe that relationship, it takes some effort to nuance which stage we are at. Moreover, there is often a blurring between the states. However, it's important to note that while the model presents the different ways we work together, and although it is presented as a continuum no inference or judgment should be made about 'progression' or 'regression', which may or may not happen due to other factors. And crucially, no state should be considered better (or worse) than another, as each has its pros and cons which may be appropriate at different times.

Caveat Emptor

In general, collaboration evangelists and many of those in favor of collaborative approaches tend to frame collaboration positively. But it is not always experienced as a positive, desirable or enjoyable experience, and there are many examples of collaborative relationships that have broken down and that require mediation or some other form of intervention. I'm reminded of some of the early work by Roger Fisher and William Ury which deals with conflict resolution—their work in this area provides many examples.[9]

---

[9] Roger Fisher and William Ury published *Getting to Yes* in 1982, a book that deals with themes such as conflict and negotiation, based on work they had been doing together since the 1970s.

One of the challenges we face when looking at collaboration models is that many depict a progression—usually from simple interaction/transaction through to co-ordination and then beyond that co-operation and ultimately on to collaboration—and imply that progression through the stages of whichever model is being shown is both linear and desirable, that is, collaboration is what we should be aiming for and that we get there having first co-ordinated well and achieved a good level of co-operation. Well, it's no surprise to learn that this isn't always the case, and many a valuable co-ordinated or co-operative effort has been destroyed through misguided attempts to force collaboration or formalize what would have been better off being left informal. As we go through the book, we will see that collaboration is highly relational. It is also complex—and it is a choice. Although I believe collaboration offers unparalleled benefits when undertaken consciously, it may not always be the most appropriate approach.

There are a number of things we can—and should—do before embarking on a collaborative venture. Colleagues at the Partnership Brokers Association and the Partnering Initiative would advocate a thorough risk assessment and investing in some form of collaboration agreement, if only to provide a basis for resolving disagreement and winding up the partnership if it doesn't bear fruit, although there are other compelling reasons for taking such a step. I explore this aspect in a little more detail in Part III of the book.

My personal experience confirms that taking the time to draw up some form of partnership—like a pre-nuptial—agreement is time well spent and speaks to the 'risk assessment' component in that it identifies potential vulnerabilities and stress-points before those aspects of the partnership find themselves being stress-tested.

Whatever you decide with regard to collaboration, it's vitally important that any relationship you establish with a partner is done with your eyes open, and that you are certain it is indeed collaboration that you seek, as opposed to a different kind of relationship.

What Can Possibly Go Wrong?

Thinking again about the initial hype and expectation, why do so many partnerships and collaborations fizzle out or evaporate?

Idealism and aiming high is no bad thing when it comes to collaborating, but it is very easy to be seduced into believing that the promise of shared equity and shared profit is the same thing as shared values and shared goals. We need to be cautious about racing ahead and hastily drawing up agreements, even when the chemistry and meeting of minds is pushing us in that direction. Although quick decisions might keep the lawyers happy and in work, we will see that there are few short cuts to creating a sustainable, successful collaboration—they are built on deeply held values, shared experience and shared understanding.

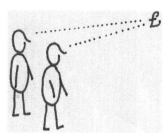

Fig. 1.2   Perceived benefit?

A collaboration that speaks only to the head, or only to the heart, may not be able to last the course. When the pressure rises, what may have once been a clear-cut case for collaboration collapses, and the trust and shared vision which is so essential for a successful partnership disintegrates.

Failing to reach agreement on the financials—the investment, the assets brought to the collaboration or created as a result, the profit—are particularly renowned for scuppering all manner of good intentions, so special care and attention should be given to these aspects. Where the motivation for collaboration is purely (or primarily) monetary, the collaboration can be unstable and susceptible to breakdown. I'm convinced that one of the reasons collaboration for social good holds so much interest and can so often be sustained is due to the higher purpose which unites diverse stakeholders around longer-term interests.

The Future for Collaboration?

As we will see in Chap. 3, the challenges our world faces today are simply not solvable by individual entities. The systems architecture and infrastructure of the world has changed; new ways of working have emerged and the role of technology and platforms have transformed the possibilities and the need for collaboration. The likelihood of any single entity having all the requisite assets, resources and stakeholder inputs to tackle the challenges our society faces is beyond remote. Rather, this is the time when government, the private sector, the public sector and civil society organizations must come together and formulate solutions.

Take for example youth unemployment, the refugee crisis, global population growth and climate change—there are many entities working on aspects of each of those challenges, but none of those issues can be tackled by a single entity, whether they may be the United Nations, the European Union, the African Union or the Arab League or a single sector. They will require academics, scientists, multinational corporations, governments and communities to come together. This requires new conscious competencies, as well as conscious effort and willpower. But there is hope: creating a better world for our children and grandchildren is pretty high up on most people's agendas, even if the incentives for action in the short term require some more work!

How to Read This Book

Business books and their readability tend to vary widely—I've endeavored to write a fast-flowing book that could easily be read on a London to New York flight. For those who prefer to dip in and out, or who have several books on the go at once, each chapter stands alone and can be read in 10–20 min, depending on your reading speed! References are listed as footnotes, and each chapter concludes with a question or two intended to prompt reflection and critical analysis.

More than anything, I hope this book can act as a sort of lens through which you are able to review, and analyze your actual and potential collaborative endeavors, as well as challenging you to reflect on your own motives and approaches to collaboration. My thoughts are born out of personal experience and my interaction with some inspiring brokers and facilitators; while I don't expect your own experience to mirror mine, I do hope that you will see enough that resonates and be able to apply some of the lessons in your own work and relationships.

For those of you who want to take the conversation further, the book's website www.consciouscollaboration.org is a great platform and offers pointers to additional resources.

Part I

The Collaboration Conundrum

Part I explores the collaboration imperative—why collaborate? And to what end? How do we know whether to collaborate, and what return could we expect? What if we're thrown into collaboration without a choice?

2

'Collaborate' or 'Fragmentate'!

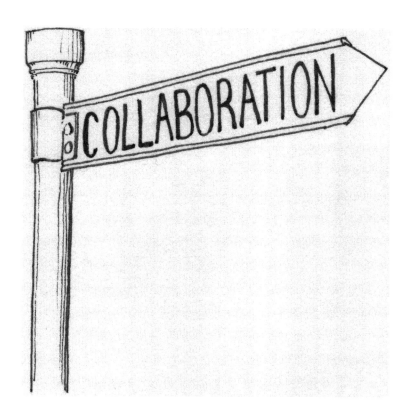

Introduction

It was Einstein who once famously said that 'we can't solve the problems we face with the same consciousness that created them.'[1] And I would say that the challenges of today, particularly the social and environmental challenges ones, truly require a different and deeper level of consciousness. One of today's most respected management voices and leader of the Future of Work Research Consortium, Professor Lynda Gratton, has spent a lot of time researching what she has coined the 'collaboration imperative',[2] and through her time spent with leading Chief Executives, influential thinkers and think-tanks such as the World Economic Forum, she is convinced that collaboration is the only hope we have.

This chapter explores the case for collaboration, the alternatives, how we might recognize an opportunity to collaborate, the returns we might expect and the resources we need to invest. It also highlights the graft and determination required to get a collaborative venture off the ground.

Why Collaborate?

We might choose to collaborate because we neither have the capacity nor the competence to tackle the challenge before us. I remember when my wife Abi and I were youth workers in our early twenties, faced with the challenge of programming activities and events for children and young people—we had no choice but to create a large team that could work together, as well as work with church groups, parents and guardians, musicians, instructors and venues, all with the purpose of providing safe, high-quality learning experiences for those in our charge. It simply would not have been possible otherwise—we couldn't have coped with the volume of work, nor provided a varied program of activities, and that was before we even had any children of our own! It reminds me of the African proverb

---

[1] This quote, and variations on it, are attributed to Albert Einstein, theoretical physicist and Nobel Prize winner.

[2] Lynda Gratton leads the Hot Spots Movement and Future of Work Research Consortium. One of the recent themes was 'the collaboration Imperative', see http://www.lyndagratton.com/Future-of-Work.html (accessed September 1, 2015).

'It takes a village to raise a child', and if ever there was a compelling case for collaboration it's in the context of raising children. We don't have to look very far to see the devastating consequences of disconnected, fragmented provision in terms of youth work, youth services and safeguarding for young people.

We might choose to collaborate because we want to create something new. As a lifelong cyclist I've been impressed by the recent example of 'Velon'[3] which provides an interesting example of how key stakeholders in cycling have come together in the interests of the sport—both the riders and the fans—and of course their own future. Speaking of the power and importance of collaboration, Sir David Brailsford, Team Director of the eponymous and successful Team Sky said:

> Collaboration is the cornerstone to positive change and as such this is very exciting for professional cycling and a big step towards the sport reaching its full potential. The teams involved in creating Velon have come together with a powerful shared vision to optimise the sport and develop new ways for professional cycling to grow. If the teams unite and work collectively with other key stakeholders to make cycling better to watch, easier to understand and get guaranteed commercial support it's to everyone's benefit and will encourage even more fans to follow the sport we love.[4]

Velon's CEO Graham Bartlett takes it further and identifies why collaboration is so important—it's all about new ideas: 'I think the way you change any business model in sport is to bring new value to the table. If you don't bring anything but want to take from what others have done, then you have a very difficult time. You have to come with new ideas.'[5]

We might choose to collaborate because what we are doing is so important it needs to scale and be adopted by as many organizations as possible, and we need as much buy-in, commitment and creativity as possible. In 2010 while I was working at People In Aid, we had an opportunity to influence the direction of the humanitarian sector by working with 19 international

---

[3] http://www.velon.cc (accessed October 1, 2015).

[4] http://www.cyclingnews.com/news/11-worldtour-teams-create-velon-business-group/ (accessed October 1, 2015).

[5] Ibid.

non-government organizations (INGOs) to create a new competencies framework. I tell the story in Chap. 6, but the point I want to make here is that in order to create something new and sustainable, which could open the way to a degree of interoperability, collaboration was the only option we had. If we went it alone, no-one would take us seriously and they would likely ignore whatever we came up with. I knew at the time it would require a great deal of energy, and sure enough it turned out to be a Herculean task, especially in the face of myriad initiatives by individual INGOs to define their own frameworks. However, the investment of energy and commitment paid off and more than 5 years later the framework has stood the test of time and been successful in guiding management and leadership development for frontline humanitarian workers.

What's the Alternative?

As with so many things in life though, we always have a choice. So, what if we choose not to collaborate? Well, it's entirely possible we could carry on independently for a long time, isolated from one another except for necessary and mundane transactions, each focused on doing our own thing… But somehow that doesn't sound very fulfilling or exciting— at least to me! And it certainly doesn't chime with the interconnected nature of life in the twenty-first century, and our interdependence. The more I think about it, the more I'm not sure it will be possible for us, or the majority of organizations and institutions, to carry on living and working in our own bubbles… We will need to make some serious choices about collaboration, or as a society we will risk fragmentation and ultimately disintegration. I think we see evidence of the seriousness of this choice in the way some industries, and in particular large multinational companies, have chosen collaboration to achieve growth, market share and profit, but where collaboration has been more challenging, particularly at a global level, we see evidence of fragmentation and possibly disintegration in areas such as transport infrastructure and systems, financial systems including taxation, public health systems and climate change.

That said, there are a few options open to us that would at face value appear to be more collaborative than individualist or isolationist, though they may fall some way short of collaboration as we have defined it. As we saw in our introduction, choosing to co-ordinate is an option that is open to us, and we could get a whole lot better at co-operating. The simple model I introduced earlier highlights the different ways in which we can work together and reminds us of the options we have, whether they be competition, co-existence, contracting, co-ordinating, co-operating, collaborating or communing.

How Do We Know When It's Time to Collaborate?

That's the 64-million-dollar question! What are the indications that we should be exploring collaboration as an option?

Perhaps we are stuck, lacking fresh ideas or creativity. Much will depend on the nature of our challenge and the outcome we seek—if we find ourselves in uncharted territory or facing an insurmountable problem, the chances are we need to think laterally and identify individuals or organizations that can help us achieve a breakthrough. That's the origin of some of the design thinking processes pioneered by organizations such as IDEO.

In international development, and particularly in the case of humanitarian responses, most interventions or programme begin with a comprehensive stakeholder analysis and needs assessment, which acts as the basis for the problem statement and the identification of desired outcomes, and these days those are the inputs which inform the theory of change. It's no coincidence that more and more humanitarian and development organizations find themselves needing to develop a partnership strategy and guidelines in order to do their work—most of the outcomes they've identified as being important are simply not achievable by a single entity. And so a key point at which collaboration could be identified as being important is at the stage of stakeholder mapping, where any gaps will emerge, and at the moment where outcomes begin to be developed.

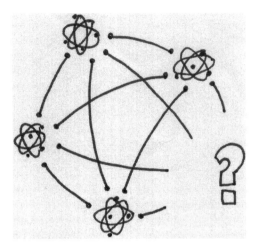

Fig. 2.1   Stakeholder mapping

What Kind of Return Can We Expect?

Measuring return on investment when it comes to collaboration is rarely straightforward: it requires a clear set of success indicators against which performance and success can be evaluated, and often requires a substantial period of time to have elapsed. And when the success is in the form of something other than a tangible asset, such as access to a community or market, or intellectual property that may be open source (as opposed to being patented) then it becomes doubly difficult.

Another way of measuring the return we might get is by looking at return on expectation, an approach or measure often used by trainers, management development experts and business schools such as the KaosPilots,[6] as an alternative to return on investment. It entails beginning with the end—the outcome—and engaging with stakeholders before, during and after, in order to assess whether expectation has been met. This could be a hard indicator, such as increased sales, a new product or lives saved, or it could be less tangible, such as engagement or satisfaction.

---

[6] The KaosPilots is an alternative business school based in Aarhus, Denmark. See http://www.kaospilot.dk (accessed October 1, 2015).

We could also think about the return in terms of social capital, which we will look at in Chap. 5. There are differing notions as to what constitutes social capital and it is still a relatively new concept that is widely interpreted—some have gone down a network mapping and analysis route (which might include number of followers and in turn their reach), while others such as LinkedIn provide a platform for individuals to leverage their connections (social capital) and convert it to the currency of web traffic, job referrals and media profile.

Collaboration in the aid sector is a long game, although increasingly the institutional funding set up is typified by short-term funding arrangements and time-bound interventions which do not favor complex collaboration, or generally allow for new, diverse partners to be brought on board.

There's another issue, too. Facilitating collaboration usually requires some specific allocation of resources (money or some other asset) to enable those collaborating to invest in the collaborative relationship. This could be as simple as reimbursing travel expenses for those who participate in joint meetings or allowing for external facilitation support from time to time, or it may involve building a website or subscribing to technological platforms that enable virtual communication and ongoing sharing of documents and knowledge. Where the resources issue is omitted or overlooked, or where insufficient funds exist to enable collaboration, then collaboration will be difficult and may even fail to materialize.

Dealing with Difference

It's not unusual to hear people say that they can't collaborate with someone and/or another organization because they simply don't get on, or because they have extensively differing goals or approaches. When this happens, it's important to dig a little deeper, as without question some of the most successful collaborations have been born from conflict and different views. The view that collaboration requires consensus and homogeneous approaches and that conflict and disagreement are to be avoided will ultimately constrain any partnership. Moreover, the behaviors that accompany such a view—false consensus, hiding from conflict—will erode the trust and limit creativity and innovation. Many experts hold the view that it is entirely possible to collaborate and yet disagree on certain aspects, sometimes fundamentally. It's taken me a while to understand this, and I'm not sure I'm completely there yet. A few years ago I remember Ros Tennyson, founder of the Partnership Brokers Association, wisely and graciously calling me out when I began 'smoothing' a conflict situation. It gave me a lot to think about—I never thought I was someone who avoided or ran away from conflict until that point, and I realized that in the heat of the moment my concern was for the group's (superficial) harmony. Instead, what was needed at the time was to surface concerns and tensions and explore them in a calm and measured way, with the aim of identifying some tangible steps forward, through, up and out of the conflict.

We'll consider the core behaviors for those who facilitate collaboration in more detail in Chap. 14, but for now it's worth noting that anyone involved in supporting and facilitating partnerships or collaborative action will quickly need to grow their confidence in negotiation, mediation and dealing with conflict situations.

Thinking back to some of the more successful collaborations, and particularly those whose outcomes have been sustained, they all have the hallmarks of having been forged through disagreement and sometimes quite vocal conflict. Our instinct tells us that great ideas benefit from being refined, yet we often fail to remember that the 'refining' metaphor involves high temperatures, agitation and careful intervention! Collaboration that is forged in the fire often endures and gives rise to great outcomes that would not have been possible otherwise.

Resources?

I've not met many people who are satisfied with the resources they have, particularly when it comes to getting a collaborative endeavor off the ground. There's never quite enough, or it's not shared, or the good times lie just around the corner. This is especially true for nonprofit organizations. Yet collaboration provides a way through this—and if we take the view that, in the spirit of William Gibson's famous quote—the resources are here but they're just unevenly distributed[7]—then our task is to identify

---

[7] https://en.wikiquote.org/wiki/William_Gibson (accessed July 1, 2015).

the assets that exist and figure out a way of leveraging those in service of our collaborative vision and desired outcome.

What resources are we talking about? Space, if our collaboration requires co-location. Money, to oil or lubricate collaborative interaction. Technology or platforms, to underpin the interaction and output. Relationships, to bring the fresh perspectives that collaboration requires.

Collaboration in the Community

A story that sticks in my mind when it comes to the hard graft required in order to open the way for collaboration comes from Action Aid in Kenya. I remember my friend Bijay Kumar, who at the time was the Executive Director, describing the challenge Action Aid faced in mobilizing women's groups and scaling community participation as part of their 'empowering women and girls living in poverty and exclusion programme'.[8] The aims were ambitious, including enabling 90,000 women and girls to challenge violence and gain political participation, working with 30 women's groups, alliances and 12 movements. Securing the participation and commitment was a long and sometimes bumpy process that required plenty of unglamorous toing and froing, preparing the way, investing in relationships and slowly building trust. Over a period of several years, and despite numerous setbacks, Action Aid was finally able to work with credibility in five programmatic areas in the west of Kenya, working at district and county level with small groups and gradually scaling up its program and achieving a number of its outcomes relating to political participation, economic empowerment and livelihoods.

What struck me was the painstaking work required and the resilience needed by those involved in the early stages. It takes determination and a relentless focus on small actions that make a difference to gradually build trust and open the way for a collaborative endeavor. It's good to be reminded that when it comes to building such a level of trust, there are few short cuts.

---

[8] http://www.actionaid.org/kenya/what-we-do/empowering-women-and-girls-living-poverty-and-exclusion (accessed April 30, 2015).

In Summary

So what have we learnt so far? I've opened by suggesting that collaboration is the only viable option for those who care about social change and tackling challenges such as climate change. I've also suggested that as the places to hide become few and far between, the alternative to collaboration is fragmentation—and ultimately disintegration. And by that I mean fragmentation of relationships, organizations and health in the widest possible sense. So, in many ways arriving at a point where we can choose to collaborate is akin to arriving at a junction. Often there are what Jeff Lucas, author and speaker,[9] calls 'junction moments', and they may be multiple. How we approach these moments is critical and we need our eyes, ears and hearts to remain open.

Collaboration isn't the easy option though, and there will be differences, disagreements and disruption along the way. Facilitating a collaboration requires patience, grace and skill—we'll return to the core competencies required in Chap. 14.

Collaboration requires resources and investment up front, as well as along the way. Whether it may be stakeholder mapping, comprehensive needs assessments or the development of clear, realistic outcomes, the costs should be calculated. However, collaboration often takes us deep into uncharted territory and it can be difficult to calculate the return on investment. I've suggested we focus on 'return on expectation' as a way of measuring the success of collaboration and we will return to this in Chaps. 15 and 16.

For Reflection

As you ponder whether you are at a 'junction moment'—whether or not to collaborate—why not take a few moments to reflect:

- What are the outcomes you seek?
- What options are open to you?
- Who are your—or your organization's—key stakeholders, and what role will they play in achieving the outcomes you seek?

---

[9] http://www.jefflucas.org (accessed October 1, 2015).

3

'Collaborative DNA?'

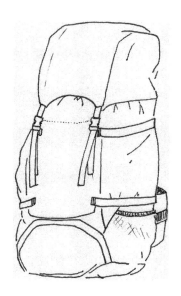

© The Editor(s) (if applicable) and The Author(s) 2016
B. Emmens, *Conscious Collaboration*,
DOI 10.1057/978-1-137-53805-5_3

Introduction

Like many who studied collaboration and partnerships, I've often wondered whether humans are hardwired to collaborate. I mean, is it fundamentally in our nature to work with others? When I was researching this book I came across a definition of collaboration in the *Urban Dictionary*. There it was defined it as 'an unnatural act practised by non-consenting adults,'[1] and this brought a big smile to my face. It certainly resonated with me and I recalled countless collaborations from the past which were precisely that! However, my recent experience has been quite different and prompted me to investigate more deeply.

As we will see, collaboration is about relationships and successful collaboration requires trust, courage, generosity, humility, expert facilitation and a truly enabling environment. Are some individuals or personalities better at collaboration than others? Is there a particular mindset that is more open to collaboration and if so what is it, and how do we recognize it or even nurture it? Are extroverts better at collaboration or more likely to initiate collaboration?

When we are able to move beyond self-interest and focus on purpose, certain behaviors appear to be unlocked. Success comes when we then surround ourselves with brilliant people—not necessarily like minds or kindred spirits, but certainly ones who are aligned with our purpose and broadly supportive of our efforts to achieve it.

This chapter explores the extent to which the desire or need to collaborate is hardwired in us—that is to say in our DNA—how different personalities approach collaboration, the mindset required for collaboration and the importance of a clear purpose and goal.

---

[1] http://www.urbandictionary.com (accessed August 1, 2015).

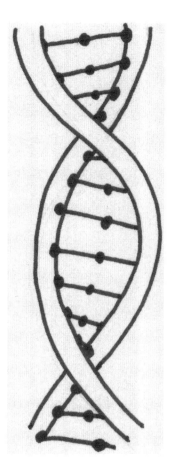

Fig. 3.1 Collaborative DNA

It's in Our Nature...

Anthropologists tell us that our species—*Homo sapiens*—is a communal species that chooses to settle and live together. From the earliest examples we have of cave paintings depicting settlements, group hunting excursions and meals shared around a fire, to research into urban communities today, we see that humans need to be around each other, with very few preferring or choosing a solitary life. Even those who retreat into the remote wilderness inevitably return to their families or loved ones at some point!

Learning from these examples, we see that in order to achieve a new goal, or create something new, many of us first look within to see what resources/capacities/competence we have and how likely we are to be able to achieve it, but we quickly move to scan our environment and identify where additional resources or assets might be, and who we can work with to achieve our goal.

Because We Had to…

Shortly after I turned 12 I remember watching a big building project take shape—it was a new house for my grandma and as children we were very excited at the prospect of her coming to live next to us. What I vividly remember about that project was the sheer number of different tradesmen who passed through and how they had to negotiate and figure out how to work together to create something new. I learned a lot of new words at that time, and there were colorful moments as carpenters, electricians, plumbers and builders disagreed and argued over small and large details, and regularly found themselves at cross-purposes. And in all that were my parents, negotiating, mediating and making decisions as best they could. Looking back now I can see there were times when it was very painful for my parents, and in many ways that is a fitting description for collaboration.

Later, with my keen passion for all things outdoors, I quickly learned that when undertaking an expedition or participating in an event such as the Ten Tors Challenge,[2] partnerships and effective collaboration between individuals were key to success. The preparation and meticulous planning were essential—hours were spent as a team poring over Ordnance Survey maps, kit lists were written and rewritten, clothing laid out, equipment

---

[2] http://www.tentors.org.uk/challenge/about (accessed August 1, 2015).

weighed and checked. And the training walks were relentless. Nothing was left to chance, despite knowing we would be at the mercy of unpredictable weather conditions and that the exertion would take us to our limits. One particularly memorable expedition involved us sharing out a team member's full kit after the first full day of walking (it was divided up equally among the remaining five team members) and all but carrying him for mile after mile as he limped on, determined to finish with the rest of us. We made it, and the sense of achievement at overcoming a challenge we thought would beat us was exhilarating!

As you might imagine, it wasn't until years later that I truly realized the level and extent of collaboration required in order to make a challenge like that happen: it took parents, teachers, instructors, the Army and a whole entourage of volunteers coming together. I note with interest now that the Ten Tors Challenge has a charter which binds that alliance together and no doubt provides the basis for some form of collaboration agreement.

Similarly, the extensive and intensive collaboration required of my family and the volunteers and employees involved in managing those early cycling races could not have been achieved without strong individual commitment to the successful outcome, and a clear and shared understanding of how all those involved would work together. People and organizations come together because they have to in order to achieve their goal. However, it has to be said that although cycle racing is important to many, the goal or outcome of such things is not really going to change this world we live in, and I soon turned my mind to thinking about whether the lessons and principles from local or small-scale collaborations could be applied more widely, and to more 'important' aspects of life.

Multidisciplinary Design: Pragmatic Collaboration

Early in my professional career I had the privilege of working for the Design Research Unit (DRU).[3] The DRU was founded in 1943 and was one of the first truly multidisciplinary design consultancies in the UK, responsible for

---

[3] https://en.wikipedia.org/wiki/Design_Research_Unit (accessed August 30, 2015).

some iconic designs including the British Rail corporate identity and elements of the 1951 Festival of Britain. Back in the 1990s one of the tasks I had was to oversee UK operations, which included managing the archives. I remember going through file after file of photos and papers describing how architects and designers came together for various projects, and documenting the design discussions that took place in the practice and with joint-venture partners. The collaborative spirit many of us tried to nurture was often challenged by demanding clients and at that time the sheer pressure of remaining solvent in a time of deep recession was a real test.

It takes a particular mindset and attitude to create a climate conducive to collaboration, and although technically brilliant, some of the characters we worked with did not seem so inclined toward nurturing the team or encouraging interdisciplinary dialogue. Factor in an international dimension (offices in Dubai, Bangkok, Kuala Lumpur and Hong Kong) and the fact that this was in the days before widespread adoption of email and internet communications (for example VOIP services such as Skype) and you had a recipe for a fair degree of tension!

Yet the clients seemed to love it. You could buy a service and benefit from the rich seam of creativity and capacity and in particular the transportation design that DRU specialized in during that period lent itself to the multidisciplinary approach whereby architects, interior architects and designers, way-finding specialists, graphic designers and corporate identity experts were able to combine to create some truly impressive integrated transport solutions in partnership with engineering firms and rail companies.

What Are the Limits?

Thinking about the networks I work with now as part of The Conscious Project—and the advice I'm often asked to give regarding how quickly to grow, what the optimum number of members is, how big should we let our consortium grow?—my mind often turns to what has been termed Dunbar's number.[4] Based on his research, Robin Dunbar, an

---

[4] https://en.wikipedia.org/wiki/Dunbar%27s_number (accessed August 30, 2015).

anthropologist, proposed that due to their cognitive limits, humans could only comfortably maintain 148 (commonly rounded to 150) stable relationships. Now the question as to whether that is true for organizations is to a large extent unanswered, although Dunbar found that Neolithic farming villages tended to number around 150 inhabitants, and that armies tended to group their basic units to a figure close to 150. In reality the number may be as few as 100 or closer to 300, and no doubt differs for each individual. However, what is interesting to us is that when we create a collaborative entity involving other organizations, we inevitably try to keep things simple and in single figures, and only gradually increase and test the limits. One network I have worked with over the last few years, the Start Network,[5] has been wrestling with this very issue as its 19 founding members decided to open the way for incremental international expansion in line with its vision and strategy. Membership discussions have centered on how equitable and meaningful participation and engagement will be enabled, and how the network's identity and core values will be upheld as the membership grows; at the time of writing there are 25 members and more growth is anticipated. The challenge lies not so much in the number of organizational members, but in the individuals within the member organizations who actually make the collaborative activity happen. Assuming each member organization has four or five individuals that regularly participate, then there are currently approximately 125 individuals involved, which means that the Director and the secretariat (approximately 12 individuals at the time of writing) already have their work cut out in maintaining the collaborative activities. This will be stretched further as the number of member organizations grows, potentially requiring a review of structure, governance and activities. Whatever happens, and regardless of what we think about Dunbar's number, the dynamic of the network and the nature of the inter-agency collaboration will continue to evolve and become more complex. Ian Gee and Matthew Hanwell's research into the workplace community is illuminating in this regard[6]: some of the issues faced by communities mirror those faced by collaborations,

---

[5] www.startnetwork.org

[6] Ian Gee and Matthew Hanwell, *The Workplace Community*, London, Palgrave Macmillan, 2015.

for example issues relating to participation, control, infighting, ensuring the right people are engaged, technology and drifting away from the original vision.

What Are the Ingredients?

This whole book is about what it takes to collaborate, or more accurately how we collaborate. To that end, each chapter identifies something of what it takes, whether it be attitude, mindset, behavior, resources, a vision or goal, a clear set of outcomes or a robust needs assessment based on sound stakeholder mapping. Successful collaboration is the result of the combination of many things, and unlike the mythical and mysterious recipe for Coca-Cola which ensures a consistent product, collaboration takes the form of a wide range of shapes and sizes, according to the partners.

In her book *The Key*,[7] Lynda Gratton explores what she termed 'collaboration tipping points',[8] citing Martin Nowak's (Harvard University) research into generosity through a game called *prisoner's dilemma* which has been used by psychologists to study co-operation. According to Gratton, Nowak found that co-operation continues as long as the percentage of those entering with self-interested rules is less than 32 % of the population. At this tipping point the community disintegrates into self-interest and co-operation is destroyed. This suggests that as long as two-thirds of the group have strong values of personal co-operation and sharing then they have a good chance of being able to carry the collaboration through the inevitable storms—but there is the potential for irreversible change to happen at the tipping point.

This serves to underline the importance of screening and selecting the right individuals to move the collaboration forward—individuals who can demonstrate collaborative competencies and who model and nurture collaborative behaviors. It also reminds us of the importance of

---

[7] Lynda Gratton, *The Key*, London, McGraw Hill, 2014.
[8] Ibid., pp. 73–74.

alignment and that when large numbers of people are involved in a collaboration things quickly become complex, and although the potential for enhanced co-operation increases, so does the risk of disintegration.

An Enabling Environment

The extent to which an environment enables collaboration is relatively unexplored in literature. There is a fair amount that talks about leadership behaviors and organizational culture, and undoubtedly these are very important. There is less, however, on the physical or environmental factors, such as workplace design, or the uptake and adoption of new technologies. A feature of much collaboration today is the fact that it is for the most part virtual. This means that leadership behaviors and the influence of leaders on the workplace is important. Although, of course, culture is inevitably shaped by all those who participate in organizational life, whether they wield hard or soft power.

I've also observed that organizations that have adopted new communications technologies early on, including collaboration platforms, are often the ones that have been successful in encouraging collaboration. Equally, organizations that have a strong oral culture (as opposed to email) and seek opportunities to physically bring their people together, are the ones that have strong internal social networks and social capital assets.

Ultimately I believe that enabling environments are created and shaped more by behaviors than by physical architecture or design, or by technology and clever gadgets! Small acts of kindness, gestures of openness, invitations and encouragement to share, non-judgmental attitudes, words of appreciation before words of criticism—all of these go a long way toward reinforcing an environment that is collaborative and enables collaborative action. But this is the hard work of self-awareness, self-reflection and self-discipline, which I admit is not always very palatable, and worse, can be risky (in that it may have unknown or unanticipated consequences).

An enabling environment is the result of people choosing to take responsibility for their self-assessment and examination seriously, and choosing to develop and maintain behaviors that enhance, promote and enable collaboration. Also—and this is much harder—it is the result of consciously reducing or limiting the behaviors that harm collaboration, even the most subtle ones! This ties in with the development and expression of collaborative values at all levels of an organization, and equally to the organizational culture. Enabling environments for collaboration are often linked to organizational cultures where personal growth is valued and encouraged, and positive changes in behavior are noticed and rewarded.

Is Collaboration Just for Extroverts?

Much has been written over the last few years championing the cause and contribution of the introvert, and how vital they are in collaborative endeavors. However, looking around, we might be forgiven for thinking collaboration was primarily the preserve of the extroverts among us! After all, aren't they are the ones who seek external stimulation, who get their energy from the outer world, and in behavioral terms, the ones often to be seen brokering new relationships and making connections with new organizations?

As with any high-performing team, a high-performing organization needs a diverse set of people to ensure success. Although extroverts may find some activities more comfortable, and some introverts may be filled with dread at the thought of being asked to collaborate with someone else, both are essential.

I'll explore in more detail later in the book, chapter 6 some of the competencies I consider to be essential when it comes to collaboration. For now suffice to say that I believe there may very well be a collaborative personality which could be profiled, and which could help us make sound recruitment and staff development decisions.

A Collaborative Mindset

Some of the most inspiring work I have come across in my career to date has been that by Carol Dweck of Stanford University on 'mindset'.[9] Her thinking about fixed and growth mindset unlocked some deep truths

---

[9] More about Carol Dweck's work on mindset can be found on her website http://mindsetonline. com (accessed September 1, 2015).

for me personally, and has a strong bearing on how we understand one another in a collaborative context.

What Dweck suggests is that in a fixed mindset, people believe that their basic qualities (such as their talent or intelligence) are fixed traits. Based on her extensive research over decades, Dweck argues that such people are likely to spend their time documenting their intelligence or talent instead of developing them. And crucially, they believe that talent alone gives rise to success, often without effort. That, affirms Dweck, is simply wrong. She goes on to suggest that in a growth mindset people believe that their basic abilities can be developed through dedication and hard work—talent might just be the starting point. Dweck is persuasive in arguing that this view (a growth mindset) creates a love of learning and a resilience that is essential for accomplishment and achievement.

For me, approaching collaboration with a growth mindset is a prerequisite. A fixed mindset is almost guaranteed to doom the collaborative venture to failure. Imagine the motivation, vision and productivity if we approach collaboration with a growth mindset, believing that anything is possible if we work hard and are open to new ideas, and to welcoming new participants in our collaboration!

So understanding Dweck's work and applying our own experience of successful collaboration helps us inch closer toward defining a collaboration mindset, and I hope that by the time we reach the end of the book we will have a much clearer idea of what that entails.

Beginning with the End in Mind

It was the management guru Stephen Covey who famously coined the phrase 'begin with the end in mind' in his acclaimed book *The 7 Habits of Highly Effective People.*[10] To my mind, that is simply one of the most profound and important things any of us can do. If we have no clear sense of purpose or goal, then we are likely to get lost along the way, or worse. Granted we can take a compass (whether literal or figurative,

---

[10] Stephen R. Covey, *The 7 Habits of Highly Effective People*, London, Simon & Schuster, 1989.

in the sense of morals, values and ethics), but without vision we will perish.

In my introductory remarks I signaled the importance of a clear outcome for any collaborative endeavor, and I can't stress that enough! It's so important to know what we're aiming for, or to be able to articulate the change we want to see happen as a result of our collaboration, or describe what we want our new product to be capable of doing.

That said, I concede that it's entirely possible to identify collaborative partners first and then through a creative process—whether design thinking or otherwise—iterate a vision and outcome that the partners can work toward. Indeed, in mature collaborations this is often how new products are created and in the context of international development and humanitarian work, it is often great minds coming together to solve a common problem that leads to the articulation of a clear and compelling vision and goal, and eventually to a set of outcomes. In our small way that is exactly how Abi and I began our own partnership and it took more than 15 years to get to a point where we were able to articulate the vision and outcomes we sought, and to be able to launch The Conscious Project. So I would say that choosing who you work or partner with is also a legitimate 'end' or goal—that is to say if the first thing you do is to decide that you want to work with the individual/s in question and there is a good fit, then provided you continue to invest in that partnership and collaborate consciously, then good things will result!

At The Conscious Project we've been inspired by a community of entrepreneurs who have connected through what is known as the Do Lectures.[11] Among the co-founders of the Do Lectures are David and Clare Hieatt, based in West Wales, and they are very clear in their own business (Hiut Denim Co.[12]) about the importance of purpose, to the extent that they are able to demonstrate that brands with a purpose do better, matter more and bring about positive change. David

---

[11] http://www.thedolectures.com (accessed August 30, 2015).

[12] http://www.hiutdenim.co.uk (accessed August 30, 2015).

Hieatt is particularly compelling when it comes to talking about the competition small organizations face when starting up, likening it to a David and Goliath situation. This got me thinking… collaboration often begins with the odds stacked against it: we hear voices saying 'it needs too much money, there's not enough time, the competition has more…', but actually the competition always has more—that's the point—so to have a chance of overcoming the competition and achieving our outcome, we have to fight differently and work differently.

In Summary

Collaboration is in our nature, and there does indeed appear to be an element of truth in the view that we are hardwired to collaborate. Some personalities seem to find it easier to connect and collaborate, but meaningful collaboration is the result of a diverse set of stakeholders agreeing to come together to achieve an outcome or create a new thing.

Collaboration thrives in environments where the human behaviors encourage and enable partnership, interaction and free exchange of views and ideas. More than whether individuals are extroverts or introverts, it is a growth mindset that is the vital, underpinning component of collaboration. The physical architecture and design can help, as can technology, but fundamentally it's the people and the human behaviors that will determine success or otherwise.

Beginning with the end in mind is probably one of the most important things we can do in a collaboration, whether your 'end' is choosing the right people or organizations to work with, or bringing diverse individuals and organizations together to work toward a common goal or outcome. In that sense, many would argue that it's also in our nature to find our purpose, so if our purpose is to bring positive social change, then we should begin by reaching out and connecting with like minds who similarly seek collaboration.

For Reflection

As you think about your own attitude toward collaboration and whether it is in your nature, why not take a few moments to reflect on:

- When have you consciously chosen to collaborate or not collaborate? Why?
- Is there a side project you'd love to work on with someone? What is it? Where does it start?
- If you seek to bring about positive social change, how can others who seek the same align their vision with yours?

4

'The Partnership Vortex'

Introduction

'The partnership vortex' is a term I coined back in 2014 while undergoing my training with the Partnership Brokers Association. It came
about as I grasped for a way to describe a situation whereby you—or
your organization—gets sucked into an uneasy or undesired partnership situation, but equally applies to forced or unequal partnerships

© The Editor(s) (if applicable) and The Author(s) 2016
B. Emmens, *Conscious Collaboration*,
DOI 10.1057/978-1-137-53805-5_4

where we might find that collaboration has been chosen for us by others. Somewhat reminiscent of the *Urban Dictionary* definition in Chap. 3—that 'collaboration is an unnatural act practised by non-consenting adults'—it's important that we acknowledge that there are times when collaboration is neither desirable, nor the answer. Yet pressure from internal or external stakeholders, and the current vogue for working collaboratively mean that there are plenty of collaborations that are unlikely to realize their potential, or for whom the writing is on the wall.

This chapter explores how a partnership vortex can arise and what we can do if we find ourselves sucked in. As we have already noted, collaboration is neither the panacea nor necessarily the desired or appropriate end state, and we need to be vigilant in ensuring collaboration is intentional *and* the right approach, as that will avoid a lot of angst and wasted resources.

What Is the Partnership Vortex?

I use the term the 'partnership vortex' as a way of describing the early stages of a 'forced' or 'unequal' partnership where the rhetoric of partnership (often used to mask what is essentially a contract or transaction), the urgency of delivery, peer pressure and the fear of missing out combine to create a dangerous whirlpool which can suck 'partners' in… Those who have the misfortune to be sucked into a partnership vortex eventually emerge battered and bruised, and while the experience can be a profound learning opportunity, more often than not it results in a breakdown of trust between 'partners' and a deep cynicism with regard to future partnerships.

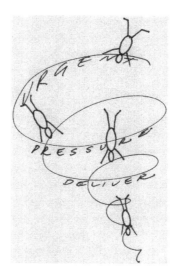

Fig. 4.1 Sucked into the partnership vortex!

In the humanitarian sector, the vortex effect often arises in complex collaborations or consortia when a large injection of upfront capital (typically from an institutional donor or investor), is channeled through a reputable (often the biggest) organization in response to a complex proposal and a commitment to deliver specific results or outcomes collaboratively. The danger of the vortex is particularly acute where 'in principle' (or binding) commitments have already been made by leadership, but the detailed processes and implementation, as well as the day-to-day management of the collaboration are delegated to management and more junior colleagues.

Dressing up legitimate contracts or transactional relationships as partnerships does a huge disservice to those brokering and building 'real' partnerships. Mutually agreed contracts and transactions are essential and often sufficient; partnerships require the risks and benefits to be shared, and a degree of equity to the way in which power and voice is distributed among partners. Contracts or transactions masquerading as partnerships take on a life and momentum of their own, creating a dangerous vortex. One thing we could each commit to is to choose the appropriate contract or relationship, and avoid turning things into something they were never meant to be.

Avoiding the vortex takes skill and sound judgment. Extricating oneself (or one's organization) from it takes courage and determination. In my experience a number of agreements need to be in place to ensure there is equity in the partnership. Time invested in defining and agreeing underpinning 'operating principles' and a collaboration agreement is well worthwhile, and we'll return to this in Chap. 5. From here, the necessary contract, Memorandum of Understanding or specific agreement can be elaborated and managed appropriately. We would each do well to re-examine partnerships we are involved in brokering, building or managing to ensure we are not at risk of being sucked into the vortex ourselves.

Choices

A basic understanding of psychology and psychometrics tells us that we each need different information or inputs in order to make a choice, and we know that the speed of decision-making will vary individually. Some collaboration gets stuck at the point of gathering information that is needed to make a choice—lost in a sea of data inputs—while other collaborations choose to proceed with incomplete or ambiguous information and their collaboration experience can be chaotic and fast-paced.

When it comes to collaborations that you or I are personally involved in, I'm guessing the reality is that relatively few of us are in the position where we get to choose who we—or our organizations—work with. And unless we are the team leader, we typically have little influence over the composition of the team and find ourselves gifted with colleagues who may or may not share our values, vision and work ethic. So, if you have ever been thrown into a collaborative endeavor with little choice, or put into a partnership situation against your will, then this book offers some pragmatic ideas that will help you navigate a way through the complexity and ambiguity, and develop collaborative relationships while maintaining your own integrity and presence of mind.

Fig. 4.2   Here is your team!

Ultimately, of course, we always do have a choice. I mean we can choose whether to stick with the job we're in or do something different, we can choose our behavior and we can choose how we use our time. But choosing does get complicated if we have dependents who we have chosen to support, or have made lifestyle choices that limit our options or require us to make compromises elsewhere. And there's some truth that making one choice can close down other choices that were previously open to us.

Love at First Sight

There are various cultural variations on the love at first sight theme, especially when it comes to corporate partnerships and collaboration. A 'let's meet for a coffee' conversation between senior executives can quickly turn into a 'let's do lunch' and before we know it, when tender documents arrive calling for a diverse or multidisciplinary team, a joint venture or joint funding proposal is hastily put together and partnerships are cemented without too much thought being given to how they will actually work if the bid is successful. Of course, those partnerships can be based on good chemistry, albeit between those responsible for business development, fundraising or marketing, rather than those who—if the tender is successful—will have to do the work together, but in this scenario the basis for collaboration is likely to be fairly superficial. Granted, due diligence may have been undertaken, but that often covers the mechanics and numbers, not necessarily the competencies or the culture and alignment, or the ability of two different organizations to work together. That presents a problem—rather like love at first sight: when the sun is shining, the weather is good and stress is manageable, it's all fine. But factor in lack of sleep, a new child or project, insecurity and external pressure or general turbulence, then the lack of a shared or sound foundation can put inordinate pressure on the relationship, perhaps causing it to crumble or break down.

I'm not saying a partnership based on good chemistry alone or created in haste cannot work—some clearly do, in a manner of speaking, just as for some love at first sight or an arranged marriage also works. But although these kind of relationships—and partnerships—can and do survive, they may never realize their full potential. Realizing potential is invariably about hard work and graft and that's as true for a relationship between two people as it is for a collaborative venture between two organizations. This gives us hope, in that although a vortex can be incredibly dangerous, it's possible to survive or extricate oneself from it by hanging on and then exerting a huge amount of energy.

A better solution is to avoid being sucked in to the vortex in the first place. But how? It's not easy to walk away from a relationship in which you've already invested. However, if the relationship turns out to be dysfunctional, exploitative or abusive, then such a courageous step may be what is required, in business as in life.

When Should We Hold Back?

A wise New Zealander once said to me that I shouldn't be afraid to trust my instinct, as the gut often has a way of telling us something we might struggle to put into words. I remember remonstrating, as I already felt I placed a fairly heavy reliance on intuition, but his argument was that it might simply be instinct drawing on 20 years' experience and that I shouldn't discount it out of hand. I often reflect on that—there is an experience gained over the years which can inform the decisions we make, or alert us to pitfalls or risks, and while I still think we should test our hunches and instincts, maybe he was right. How many times have you been presented with an opportunity to work together on a project but something is niggling you. Perhaps a question about whether promised resources will materialize or a doubt about commitment. We need to pay attention to all the information coming our way, and this is especially true when it comes to partnerships. In the giddy enthusiasm and fresh optimism that typifies the early stages of any relationship, we need to be sure to ask the right questions. Of course, it's possible for our spirit to be crushed—whether through getting bogged down in a lengthy due-diligence process that saps energy or becoming lost in figures, policies and protocols. The trouble is, intuition is not easily quantified as a competence—or certainly not in a way that we can consistently measure or develop. So let us give space at the outset, or in the early stages of a partnership, for questions and concerns to be aired honestly and openly, so that the risk of being sucked into the partnership vortex is minimized.

Warning Signs

What are some of the signs that we might need to hold back, or ask some direct questions? They could be many, and it could be simply a hunch. Practically, the warning signs may manifest as a misalignment in terms of vision, a disconnect in terms of values, unequal distribution of resources, insufficient investment in the partnership, unequal profit or proceeds, arguments or heated discussion about the end goal or time required to achieve it or questions over outcomes and their sustainability.

Fig. 4.3   Heed the warning signs!

Asking the Questions

The best way of raising concerns is through decent open questions, and some scenarios or 'what if?' questions. What if our collaboration attracts three or four times as much investment as we need, what would we do then?

I recently came across an example of a potential partnership where I felt caution needed to be exercised. It related to the development of new strains of seeds (including rice and grains). The nonprofit organization in question was committed to an open-source solution where the intellectual property was in the public domain and accessible by farmers and growers of all sizes, but needed to work with the private sector to achieve the scale and reach desired by institutional donors. Yet the work was being done at the same time as a large private company working on similar issues was filing various patents for new gene sequences and suing farmers for patent infringement. To my mind that created a complicated basis for a partnership. The challenges were not insurmountable, but they required a lot of discussion and negotiation and there was no guarantee of a successful partnership at the end of all that. Some partnerships simply may not be compatible or able to work due to conflicts of interest.

But there are examples of some quite striking partnerships that have been successful in the world of international development, although both insiders and outsiders have asked many questions. For example the successful partnership between Save the Children and GlaxoSmithKline, which at the time of writing has funded training for over 5000 health workers across West and Central Africa, Sudan, Haiti and Yemen.[1] Or the collaboration between Nestlé and the Fairtrade foundation which has received widespread praise.[2] (Along with a fair amount of criticism largely based on its critics' beliefs that it is not doing enough in terms of fair trade, and has still not addressed concerns about the way in which its markets infant formula.)

---

[1] http://www.savethechildren.org.uk/about-us/who-we-work-with/corporate-partnerships/our-partners/gsk (accessed September 30, 2015).

[2] http://www.fairtrade.net/single-view+M5ef75ffaaeb.html (accessed October 1, 2015).

What Are the Options?

In the Introduction I presented the collaboration continuum, which acts as a framework to help us codify a range of relationships. The model doesn't suggest a hierarchy of importance and isn't intended to support a linear progression through a series of stages or steps toward collaboration and ultimately community—rather it indicates various types of relationship, each of which has its own merits and which may be entirely appropriate and sufficient at a given moment.

There's no need to make your working relationship into something it is not! Looking again at the model, we can ask ourselves whether we are trying to force a collaboration when it isn't necessary, or whether external pressures, or the 'optics', are pushing us to collaborate but in reality it's not the best option for the partners at that time. Knowing where we are or being able to discern where we are is important and may help us identify when we are at risk of being sucked into the partnership vortex.

Courage to Challenge

Having the courage to challenge is a key competence for leaders and I will expand on this in Chap. 14. But it's also relevant here because it's in the early stages where courageous and fair challenges are so important. There are two issues for me here: (1) having the courage to challenge, and (2) equally important, knowing how to raise the challenge in a constructive and open way. When trust is still quite fragile, how we raise questions, concerns and challenge assumptions is critical. Assumptions are the enemy of communication and understanding—and all too often it's easier to 'go with the flow' or 'not rock the boat' than to take stock and ask a difficult question.

Having the courage to challenge is a competence that executives and partnership brokers need to improve. We need to understand some of the intercultural issues at stake here, too. For example, how power is seen by the culture we're in—who can legitimately raise questions, who can challenge, and how the challenge is dealt with. My advice to those who find themselves brokering or facilitating a collaboration is to design in time and space for challenge, and to script some questions that depersonalize the issue substantially. Appreciative spaces and reflective spaces at intervals allow for individuals to air concerns they may have. Simple questions and encouraging simple language help cut through jargon and clichés that may be hiding or masking potential issues. Individuals can be invited to summarize the issues for the rest of the group or play out the role of a new stakeholder or recipient, with the mandate to ask any question they want.

In order to get on track, the questions do need to be asked, but people and relationships need to be handled sensitively, especially in the early stages where there is a lot to lose. In a potentially unequal partnership—which by the way can turn out to be an effective and high-performing collaboration—extra care needs to be taken when challenging the thinking of the collaboration.

Storming

As my friend Ros Tennyson says, disagreement in a partnership is not a bad thing or something to be avoided! This is hard for someone who prefers folk to get along happily and debate constructively and politely. Chaotic, noisy negotiation and bargaining convey a sense of confusion and can be messy—I'm sure I'm not the only one who prefers my anarchy to be neat and orderly, with all challenges rational, measured and evidence based. But we need the mess and often it's unavoidable. As I say to my children 'making things is messy' and this is so true for a collaboration that is making something new for the world. We should not be frightened of what the psychologist Bruce Tuckman termed 'storming',[3] a stage that every team has to go through in order to perform, and I think we can apply this to the 'team' that comes together as part of a collaboration.

---

[3] Bruce Tuckman, Stages of group development (1965). Available at: https://en.wikipedia.org/wiki/Tuckman%27s_stages_of_group_development (accessed October 5, 2015).

Exiting Humanely

On occasions, partnerships to need to be terminated, or one of the parties to a collaboration will need to withdraw. In relatively small industries or market sectors, such as international development, how the exit process is managed becomes quite important. Here there is learning to be gained. As with the exit of an employee, the manager never quite knows if the next time they encounter that individual he/she will be a client, a donor or indeed a more senior manager, so for this reason alone it is worth investing consciously and carefully in the transition; it always pays to manage exits and transitional moments with integrity and in a humane manner. This goes for partnerships and collaborative ventures, too. Perhaps it's the HR Director in me but I would maintain that any termination should be preceded by a clear—and as far as possible transparent—process which gives all sides an opportunity to say their piece, reach the right decision in the circumstances and then move on.

I'm increasingly of the view that we could and should do more in terms of dignity in the workplace. By that I mean actually living and acting with respect, as opposed to pointing to respect as a corporate value, and then doing what we wanted to do anyway—often without respect and without a view to the future or wider implications—and the inevitable unintended consequences that accompany our decision and action. So what that translates to in an exit procedure is simple unemotive language, a recognition of incompatibility on this occasion or honest acknowledgment of behaviors that were not sufficiently demonstrated and then moving on.

There can be other consequences to an exit though—over and above a loss of face are details such as legal fees and compensation. That's why collaboration and entering into a partnership is not something to be taken lightly; it needs careful forethought and we shouldn't trivialize the attention to detail required. The notion of a partnership prenuptial which I mentioned in the Introduction isn't so far-fetched after all—a clear process for dissolving or winding up and dispersing any assets could come in very handy if things don't turn out according to plan.

In Summary

The risk of being sucked into a partnership vortex is very real, and we need to be alert to the likelihood and aware of the consequences. Collaboration offers real benefits but is not always appropriate, feasible or possible. At the outset we do well to consider the options we have and whether there is a better—more appropriate—framework for the relationship we are entering into. 'Let's do business' may simply require a contract for services or a straightforward transaction and thus a lot of heartache and pain could be saved. Collaboration works best when it is 'conscious', that is to say when those collaborating agree to do so and mutually consent, and where there is mutual interest, mutual respect and a common goal. Getting to that point requires open eyes and honest communication, and that in turn requires courage and integrity. This doesn't mean collaboration is plain sailing, or all about flowers and chocolates! Collaboration entails hard graft and commitment, as well as the resilience to see through the storms and weather robust debate and disagreements to achieve the desired goal.

For Reflection

As you think about the partnerships you have established, and collaborations you've been involved with, why not take a few moments to reflect:

- Which of the collaborations that are you involved in could be better described by a term other than partnership?
- Which of your existing collaborations would benefit from being reframed?
- How prepared are you in the event that you need to exit a partnership or dissolve a collaborative venture?

5

'Collaborative Capital'

Introduction

Without a doubt, I believe one of the most important aspects of collaboration is our collaborative capital, by which I mean primarily our 'social capital'—what it is, how we measure it, how we choose to invest it and how we can increase it. My belief is born out of my experience that everyone always has something they can contribute, no matter how large or small. As with pot luck lunches where individuals each bring an offering for the larger group, and somehow it works, so it can be with collaboration. However, there is certainly benefit to a degree of co-ordination.

© The Editor(s) (if applicable) and The Author(s) 2016
B. Emmens, *Conscious Collaboration*,
DOI 10.1057/978-1-137-53805-5_5

This chapter explores the notion of social capital, how it relates to collaboration and how it can be invested. In a collaborative context, stakeholders bring their 'assets' by way of investment in the collaboration, as well as their expectations. These contributions, investments, or expectations usually cost something, and so it is important to determine whether there is a return, profit or some other benefit as a result.

What Do I Mean by Social Capital?

In one of my previous roles as a leader in a global network of more than 200 NGOs, I had an opportunity to connect people, and to play my part in bringing about transformational results for the organizations we worked with and the communities they served. And that's what's got me thinking about relationships and 'social capital'… what is our social capital, how do we invest it and what is the return on that investment or the return on those relationships? Is our social capital the sum of our 'connectedness'/relationships, and our behaviors/attitudes? That could be a useful starting point…

Those who are renowned for working collaboratively typically use their convening 'power' (or social capital?) to create and nurture community, and to facilitate virtual and face-to-face interaction and learning. When this power is aimed at improving the way in which the humanitarian and development community works to overcome poverty and alleviate suffering around the world, it's similar to the act of investing social capital—that is the sum of our connectedness/relationships, and our behaviors/attitudes—for good, or even for social profit.

Some organizations have begun to use network mapping techniques, such as Social Network Analysis,[1] to map and analyze what is to all intents and purposes social capital, presenting them in the form of sociograms. The mapping typically entails recording the incidence and frequency of relationships and interactions between what are termed 'nodes' (they could be people, organizations or things). Tools from network theory can then be used to identify key individuals, organizations or communities, as well as robustness or structural stability in a network, and naturally this can be used for both good and less good purposes.

---

[1] https://en.wikipedia.org/wiki/Social_network_analysis (accessed September 1, 2015).

Investing and Depositing Social Capital

The concept of making a deposit in a bank account is helpful as we seek to understand flows of social capital. Stephen Covey used a similar metaphor when describing trust (which we will come to again in Chap. 12). The principle is that multiple down-payments made diligently over time create an asset that can be drawn down when needed. The question is when and how can we best make these deposits? And what do they look like?

One idea I have is based on an experiment I began many years ago. I decided that whatever industry or sector I ended up working in, I would make it my business to read voraciously—anything to do with work—and rather than simply store that knowledge and the insights gained, I would commit to sharing them widely. I would distribute by email or use a platform like Twitter to share links with colleagues, co-workers, collaborators and clients. No doubt it helped to be a fast reader, but what really mattered what the process of curation that was taking place. Sharing generously through gratuitous acts of kindness was appreciated, and over time people would contact me asking whether I had read anything or knew anyone who was writing about a topic of relevance. The logical extension for me was then connecting people. By taking care to introduce people with similar interests or concerns and let them figure out what the next steps were, I somehow benefitted. Maybe not through a direct return from those I helped or introduced, but through others who would take time to introduce me to interesting people or share something they'd been reading. Looking back I can see that in a small way, these were investments and deposits of social capital.

What Holds Us Back?

I suppose one of the things that holds us back is fear. Fear that we might be relinquishing an advantage, or handing over information that will compromise us. The old adage of knowledge being power may be a truism but it is still significant. Giving something away theoretically means we no longer have it. That's not strictly speaking true in the case of knowledge or a connection—we may still hold that knowledge, or still be connected to an individual. So we could reframe that for ourselves.

Another thing that might hold us back is our application of policy, for example our obedience to HR policies and procedures and a desire to look busy. Time spent networking, brokering introductions or acquiring knowledge that we may or may not be able to apply is not really the stuff that gets rewarded by an organization, however relevant it may turn out to be later on.

Sometimes there may be legal reasons holding us back—perhaps we've been required to sign nondisclosure agreements or confidentiality clauses. And it's true that those can mitigate the free flow of social capital.

In general, social and collaborative capital tends to be developed by those who venture and risk, and much less so by those who hold back or hedge their investments.

Setting the Tone

Organizational culture is often credited with encouraging or blamed for discouraging collaboration. Can it be true that culture is such an important factor? This isn't a book about organizational culture, but it's true that we can't really explore how a collaborative environment is created and nurtured without touching on it. If culture is at its simplest 'how we do things around here',[2] then that places a huge responsibility on organizational leaders and those who manage—something we'll come back to consider in more detail in Chap. 14. Crucially, it is those who—in the words of my friend and coach Rajan Rasaiah—'set the tone' that have an enduring responsibility and, whether they like it or not, it is they who model the behaviors for the majority.

Organizations that have nurtured a learning economy, whereby discoveries and learning are freely shared, genuinely appreciated and constructively critiqued, will be the ones at the vanguard of a collaborative economy. I've seen countless examples of a simple internal collaboration begin with the open question 'How can I help you?' and from those humble beginnings some incredible breakthroughs have emerged. It takes courage to ask that kind of a question, and grace to answer it. But as with

---

[2] David Drennan, *Transforming Company Culture*, London, McGraw Hill, 1992. Cited by Andrew Brown, *Organisational Culture*, London, *Financial Times* and Prentice Hall, 1995, p. 8.

trust, each interaction around that type of question is a small deposit in the trust bank and can be drawn down at a future point.

An organizational culture in which individuals and/or departments openly barter or exchange resources is also one that creates a climate in which collaboration can thrive, often between unusual suspects. I've witnessed this recently through the medium of Action Learning Sets,[3] which I and colleagues have been facilitating for the Scout Association as part of a substantial investment in leadership development. In an Action Learning Set, after a round of bidding, each individual in turn brings a real issue to the set and it is discussed and debated. Often the issues brought are particularly difficult or knotty, and ones that an individual has simply been unable to give time to as part of their everyday job. What I've noticed is that often in the wrap-up a number of unsolicited offers are made, which the presenter is free to take or leave. Of itself that is not particularly remarkable but what has been interesting—and of huge benefit to the organization—is that those offers have been taken up, and it is that openness and generosity which has been central to some of the more complicated and complex issues being partially or wholly resolved. How did that come about? It's hard to put a finger on it—is it the way in which the set was facilitated? Is it the individuals themselves and the fact they come from different departments? Is it the nature of the issues being discussed? Is it the organizational culture? No doubt it is some of all the above, although what is certain is that the set itself has developed its own culture, based on trust built and time invested, and collaborative capital acquired. As a result they and the organization have reaped the benefits.

Modeling Collaborative Behavior

Building on the importance of setting the right tone, the way in which each of us models collaborative behavior carries much more influence than we might imagine. We've touched on various acts and behaviors

---

[3] Action Learning is based on a concept that individuals learn best from self-assessment and personal reflection. It is attributed to Reg Revans who developed it in the 1940s, describing it as a social exchange in which managers learn with and from one another during the diagnosis and treatment of real problems. Reg Revans, *ABC of Action Learning*, Gower, 1983.

already: often we only recognize collaborative behavior when it's absent, or when we're confronted by behavior that is blatantly anti-collaborative. What do I mean by that? It could be as simple as individuals not listening to one another, or it may be acts of selfishness or self-interest, undermining words and lack of recognition for someone else's effort or achievement.

Sometimes it's more innocuous, but equally frustrating—such as the networker who thrusts a business card into your (and everyone else's) hand at the business event, with no thought as to the relevance of their services to you and even less regard for the value or relevance of your services to them. That kind of behavior stands in great contrast to careful, active listening and thoughtful introductions to people who in turn can connect open people with others.

Leaders have the chief responsibility when it comes to modeling collaborative behavior and I'll expand on this in Chap. 14. For now though, if I had to offer a guiding principle it would be based on the golden rule: 'we should treat others in the way we want to be treated ourselves'.

What's the Secret to Increasing Collaborative Capital?

I would say it's in the small acts of openness and kindness—taking time to extend ourselves beyond our own bubble and being open and receptive. We'll look at generosity in much more detail in Chap. 7 as I believe it is fundamental to a collaborative culture and developing collaborative capital. And as we get further into the book we'll also explore the notion of boundary spanning and how this behavior is inextricably bound up with increasing collaborative capital.

Space to Collaborate?

I mentioned earlier the way in which some organizations have made counter-intuitive decisions in this age of austerity by investing in their offices, shared spaces and amenities for staff to enjoy. Some of the largest firms in the world have done this, creating campus-style sites for work and learning, and they claim it not only increases employee engagement but productivity, too. Having looked at the evidence over the years, and taking into account sickness absence and the impact of a highly engaged workforce, I personally am convinced, though it would take a brave nonprofit organization to make a similar investment. Even if they do invest in say, a canteen or basic recreational space, it is very rare to see gyms, swimming pools and entertainment facilities, particularly in locations where the price of real estate is high, or the local media are renowned for their critical view of such amenities. What I've experienced when working with nonprofit organizations in such an environment—particularly working in a campus environment in sub-Saharan Africa or in southern Asia—is the space for human interaction and sharing of knowledge and experience. It's not all about extravagant investment in an employee experience though—simple elements that are 'designed in' can go a long way, as the example of Oxfam shows, below.

In the early days following Oxfam GB relocating its UK head office to a contemporary building in a business park, I often visited and would bump into many different contacts in the central atrium area and in the cafeteria, and valuable conversations would ensue. For a network organization (which I represented) those public spaces were a very productive place to do business and many of the humanitarian projects I was responsible for were nudged forward through timely conversations and by being able to negotiate project contributions or commitments. It's much harder to plan for serendipitous encounters when decision makers remain in their cubicles or hidden away on the upper floors, and careful thought to the design and layout of the physical space can pay dividends.

As we see then, the physical space we inhabit has a bearing on collaboration and collaborative culture. Dilbert-style cubicles, closed offices, a small reception area and no central space to eat or have downtime create a very different environment than one that has a well-run staff canteen, lounge areas, a roof terrace and decent coffee. People will say that one of the things I'm known for is good coffee and in an office that often equated to a good supply of fresh ground beans and a cafetière which would be shared with the team and visitors alike. Not because coffee is the only aid to creative thinking and problem solving (though I often joke that it is the most important fuel for any entrepreneur!), but because in that act of creating space to slow down, enjoy a slow coffee, reflect and have a conversation, the collaborative work could continue.

That's all well and good when a team is co-located, but what about geographically dispersed teams or remote teams which are increasingly the norm for the nonprofits I work with? Not to mention the escalating cost of real estate forcing organizations to review whether they can afford space for a canteen or breakouts.

Another issue with compartmentalized spaces is that they can have the downside of reinforcing existing (closed) networks or limiting them to those who can participate. Moreover, some business models mean that folk never get to see each other and this calls for creativity. I remember once visiting an organization and walking past a projected (live) image of another office with people busily working away. Every so often someone would turn to the camera and wave or hold up a note... It looked quite fun, so I asked about it. It turned out that it was a live webcam in the other UK office in the north of England. One way the leadership team felt they could maintain a connection between the spaces was to play a live feed via webcam of the main working offices. Interesting, and imaginative!

Much has been made of the rise of the virtual watercooler, whether it be Skype or some other technology. It's true they play an important role in facilitating connections and increasingly we have to think laterally and imaginatively as our workplaces change and the way we work evolves.

Risk

The risk of a loss when it comes to social capital is real—and equally the value of the investments we make can go down as well as up. We are prone to making poor judgments or misjudgments, and circumstances can change quickly. Brilliant collaborative ideas can quickly fizzle out— through lack of investment or resources or sometimes because they are doused or extinguished by another source, or simply starved of oxygen in the day-to-day activity of organizational life.

How can the risk be mitigated? Long-term deposits? Spread betting? There seems to be sense in playing the long game and if we apply the metaphor—that is, we are clear about our vision and long-term outcomes—then that can guide the way we invest and develop the social capital we have. In that sense our action is not so different to us treating our social capital as venture capital: where investment decisions are underpinned by appropriate due diligence and we stick with the investment through the ensuing ups and downs as we track toward our intended outcome.

Notwithstanding the considerable risks, there are practical steps we can take in mitigation. These include insisting on a collaboration agreement, long promoted by organizations like the Partnership Brokers Association, and if that doesn't encompass all the behaviors we expect, then we can also take the step of negotiating and agreeing some 'operating principles' that can guide the behavior and interaction between parties to a collaboration. We'll come back to the subject of the collaboration agreement and operating principles in Chap. 15.

Personally, I'm a fan of agreeing simple operating principles and putting in place a transparent collaboration agreement. It is possible to leave the development of social capital to chance, or even to the market, and let a collaborative venture run its natural course, but I'm not convinced that is in the collective interest, especially when we want or need to leverage our social capital for the success of the collaboration.

In Summary

We each have social capital which we can bring to a collaboration and in essence this is what we might term collaborative capital. How we develop it and how we choose to invest it are deeply personal choices, although we must recognize that those around us are watching carefully to see what we do. The level of scrutiny varies according to our profile, and with more responsibility comes greater expectation and requirements. Leaders are responsible for setting the collaborative tone and whether (or how) they choose to model collaborative behaviors will have a profound influence on the collaborative culture of an organization.

There are practical steps we can take to mitigate the risks associated with investing our collaborative capital, from agreeing operating principles to drawing up collaboration agreements. Organizations can also choose the extent to which they might design collaborative workspaces that encourage or promote social interaction and collaborative conversations, although in cost-conscious times nonprofit organizations may be more limited than their for-profit counterparts. Whatever is chosen, a whole cost/whole investment versus return on investment calculation must be made as the return from a highly engaged, collaborative workforce is not to be underestimated. Depending on how an organization works, it may be that a collaborative workspace pays for itself in a relatively short period of time.

For Reflection

As you consider your social capital, why not take a few moments to reflect on:

- How you can convert your social capital to collaborative capital?
- How you could nurture or develop collaborative capital further?

Part II

Conscious Collaboration

Part II takes us to the heart of the matter—conscious collaboration.
Here we will consider some of the core behaviors required for conscious collaboration, explore how and where conscious collaboration happens and what we can do to encourage and enable it.

6

'Conscious Collaborators'

The closer we look at collaboration, the more it becomes apparent that the real issue is not really *whether* we work together, but *how* we work together. Part I put forward the argument for collaboration—the collaboration imperative—and there is little doubt that collaboration and rethinking the way we work together is one of the most pressing issues of the decade, if not the twenty-first century. Whether we find ourselves collaborating in teams, across departments, between organizations or with

© The Editor(s) (if applicable) and The Author(s) 2016
B. Emmens, *Conscious Collaboration*,
DOI 10.1057/978-1-137-53805-5_6

different sectors and industries, how we go about collaborating is the question on everyone's lips.

Unlocking the potential that collaboration offers requires a set of behaviors that are in many ways counter-cultural and counter-intuitive. Our world would be a very different place if we took the view that most people are generally good, yet many think, act and work from a position of fear and self-interest. Politicians and the media are often held up as being among the worst offenders, but at some point most of us choose to act according to our own self-interest, and when self-interest takes over the collective interest, then collaboration often falters.

This chapter begins by identifying some of the core competencies for collaboration in the twenty-first century. We'll come back to the issue of leadership behaviors in Chap. 14.

Competencies: A Word of Warning

Before we dive into competencies in more detail, I need to give one caveat. Competencies for many people, particularly those working in HR or in management positions, evoke a mixed bag of emotions—not all of them pleasant. Many HR colleagues in the nonprofit organizations I have spent time with over the last 15 years describe how they have struggled to get competencies and competency frameworks understood and adopted, despite the fact that as a concept and management tool, they have gradually become more mainstream since their introduction at the end of the 1980s. Many frameworks developed in the 1990s and early 2000s were cumbersome and unwieldy, and it's fair to say a few executives lost faith in their HR counterparts and struggled to see the relevance of the frameworks. However, I saw this begin to change about 10 years ago, certainly in the aid sector, and various initiatives were launched in an effort to get the benefits understood and accepted. And to a large extent, those efforts have been successful—there is no longer a rolling of eyes when competency-based recruitment is discussed with a recruiting manager, management behaviors are evaluated on a more routine basis and frameworks for professional development and recognition have sprung up all over the place, and not just in academic institutions. It's rare today for me to come across an organization that has not developed a basic competencies framework, even if it is just for their senior staff and executive team.

One thing that has evolved over the last 15 years is the received understanding and definition of what competencies are. Traditionally understood to be knowledge, skills and attitudes, we find that today they are more widely understood to be the behaviors required to perform effectively,[1] or to quote the Chartered Institute of Personnel and Development:

> The terms 'competency' and 'competencies' focus on the personal attributes or inputs of an individual. They can be defined as the behaviours (and technical attributes where appropriate) that individuals must have, or must acquire, to perform effectively at work.[2]

That evolution has, to my mind, been instrumental in helping competencies regain acceptance and in extending the focus from technical competencies to what are sometimes referred to as management and leadership competencies or behaviors. My preference is to refer to them as management and leadership behaviors, rather than 'soft skills' as I am aware some do!

Core Humanitarian Competencies Framework: A Breakthrough

Back in 2010 I had an opportunity to play a leading role in the development of a core competencies framework for the humanitarian sector.[3] As with many such pieces of work—I and others had spent years pushing for greater recognition of the contribution a clear framework could make, but with the vagaries of funding in the humanitarian system I hadn't

---

[1] The Chartered Institute of Personnel and Development (CIPD), http://www.cipd.co.uk/hr-resources/factsheets/competence-competency-frameworks.aspx (accessed October 1, 2015).

[2] Ibid.

[3] http://www.start-network.org/wp-content/uploads/2014/01/Core-Competencies-Framework.pdf and http://www.start-network.org/wp-content/uploads/2014/01/Core-Humanitarian-Competencies-Guide.pdf (both accessed April 1, 2015).

really had the opportunity to consolidate that thinking in any way other than working with committed individuals, interest groups and the occasional organization, to publish a few papers and reports, and run some workshops for more progressive aid agencies. The interest bubbled away, and a small number of interested folk remained in contact, watching for a moment to seize and then move the discussion and debate forward by a few more steps. As is often the way, I found myself busy with other useful things, but then the moment came along at relatively short notice, requiring some swift decision-making and even swifter action.

It was clear from the initial contact that here was an opportunity to move forward by more than a few steps—with the right partners it felt as though we could transform the debate and achieve a real breakthrough. But it was going to take a huge amount of work, a massive vision and sheer determination to see it through. Not everyone was convinced it would be possible. Years later I remember a conversation with one INGO's Humanitarian Director who confided that he was convinced it (agreeing a core competencies framework between 19 leading humanitarian organizations) could never be done, and at the time he had chosen to bite his tongue hard, and simply go along with the process. I was glad he did go along with it, even if it was perhaps a half-hearted or hedged commitment. I wonder how many others felt that way? Even now that episode gives me deep insight into what can make or break collaboration. Sometimes we need to go with the flow and not obstruct the energy of a few committed visionaries. In fact more than that, sometimes we need to deliberately choose to 'hold back' in order to see the direction, the resources being leveraged and the opportunities emerging.

Going back to the story and how we managed to develop and agree the framework, there are three aspects that stand out as being noteworthy and characteristic of a successful collaboration. First, the partnership between my then employer People In Aid and the lead humanitarian agency Action Aid—and in particular the partnership between my boss, People In Aid's Executive Director, Jonathan Potter, myself and the then Head of International Humanitarian Action and Resilience Team, Bijay Kumar— was built on a foundation of robust and open communication and characterized by some fairly frank exchanges about the desired outcome, proposed processes, the risks, and the budget and timeline. They—Action Aid and the consortium of 19 organizations—believed in us, and we trusted them to honor their commitment and work with integrity. While the outcome was clear we were able to help challenge their thinking, and then together develop and define a collaborative process that recognized where decision-makers were situated, but allowed for wide participation by stakeholders at all levels.

Second, I was fortunate and able to quickly bring on board one of my long-time collaborators, Sara Swords, whose consultancy skills, subject matter expertise and international facilitation experience was exactly what we needed. Together, along with my Executive Director's full support and affirmation and the client commitment, we were able to propose a participatory process for the development of a framework that the 19 consortium members would feel able to adopt.

Third, over the years both Sara and I and those involved in the project team had acquired a large amount of social capital, to the extent that when we put out the word about the work we were doing we were able to reach out to our networks and draw on established relationships and connections based throughout Europe, the USA, Africa, Asia and Australasia in order to ensure our work and thinking reflected a much bigger picture.

Sara and I were very clear that the process was not about any single organization and nor was it about us having an opportunity to demonstrate any particular skill. What we were able to successfully convey was that the opportunity we had was an unprecedented one and that it offered us an opening to influence change and act in the interests of those the humanitarian organizations served—that is the disaster- and conflict affected-people.

As a process, it was ambitious and involved simultaneous workshops in London and Nairobi, digital engagement and lots of drafting and redrafting, negotiating and testing. Our hope was that it might provide a basis for organizations to then develop their own bespoke frameworks. Our intent was that it would underpin the management and leadership development programs that were being developed at the time, and guide capacity strengthening investment in the core skills of humanitarian workers around the world.

It turned out to be one of the most successful things I've ever been involved in, and at the time of writing the framework is recognized by many international and local humanitarian NGOs, by the International Federation of Red Cross and Red Crescent Societies, by UN agencies such as UN OCHA, the World Food Programme and UNICEF and by academic institutions. The next stage for the framework will be the development of appropriate levels and more detailed indicators. Competency frameworks are dynamic and their evolution should be encouraged in order to meet the changing requirements of the future world of work.

Collaborative Behaviors?

If we are to succeed in identifying and developing collaborative potential, then we need to be a lot more specific about the behaviors that are required for effective collaboration. This isn't as easy as it sounds, but based on the pioneering work we undertook with the consortium of humanitarian agencies, I'm going to have a go at proposing a few. I'm convinced that the learning from the aid sector applies just as much to other sectors, although of course it's not the only sector which relies on collaboration to achieve its goals, and I'd be the first to say there's a whole lot more learning about collaboration that needs to be done within the aid sector, too.

That said, the easiest (and perhaps least contentious) place to start is by identifying the main areas in which behavioral indicators can be developed. For me, the core behaviors that are absolutely key cover four areas, captured by the following headings:

1. Listening and dialogue
2. Working with others
3. Self-awareness
4. Critical judgment
    And if I were to suggest a fifth area it would be:
5. Motivating and influencing others

There are no doubt other areas of competence that are important, and you might be thinking I've missed a crucial heading. If that's the case then I hope as time goes by we'll have an opportunity to discuss and develop these ideas further. We should note that technical competencies for collaboration are becoming increasingly important. By technical competencies I mean areas such as digital literacy, and I will return to this in Chap. 14 and offer a few more suggestions. I also think there is an area of overlap with the competencies required for effective facilitation and partnership brokering, and I will touch on this toward the end of this chapter.

For now, let's look at the core behaviors I'm proposing in a little more detail:

1. Listening and dialogue
   There are two critical behaviors here:

   * Actively listen to different perspectives and experiences of stakeholders
     And the second is especially important for those working in the aid sector:
   * Establish and maintain clear communication and dialogue with stakeholders

   Both these behaviors include personal active listening skills and also the ability to use mechanisms and communication structures for engagement with stakeholders, including being able to communicate in the preferred language of stakeholders and faithfully and non-judgmentally reflect their views and perspectives. An additional behavior under the heading listening and dialogue is: ensuring feedback from partners and other stakeholders is incorporated into program design, planning and learning.

2. Working with others
   At its simplest and most basic, collaboration is working with others. This requires all individuals involved in the collaborative activity to:

   * Contribute positively in the team to achieve program objectives.
   * Share useful information and knowledge with colleagues, partners and other stakeholders as and when appropriate.
   * Actively participate in networks to access and contribute to good practice.

- Challenge decisions and behavior which breach any codes or the collaboration agreement.

We've already touched on the importance of having courage to challenge—so for the last bullet point in the above list we should take as a given that successful collaboration requires individuals to be able to challenge decisions or behavior that breach any Codes or statutes that apply.

When we were working with our consortium of INGOs we went further here, and began drafting behaviors that we would expect to see at the next level, that is those being demonstrated by first level managers. These included a requirement for individuals to:

- Establish clear objectives with teams and individuals
- Monitor work progress and individual performance.
- Establish agreed ways of working at a distance with partners and staff.
- Work with your team to build trust with communities and stakeholders.
- Foster collaborative, transparent and accountable relationships through partners to formalize and implement partnering agreements.
- Use negotiation and conflict resolution skills to support positive outcomes.

3. Self-Awareness

- Show awareness of your own strengths and limitations and their impact on others.
- Demonstrate understanding of your skills and how they complement those of others to build team effectiveness.
- Seek and reflect on feedback to improve your performance. </BPL>

4. Critical Judgment

- Analyze and exercise judgment in challenging situations in the absence of specific guidance.
- Demonstrate initiative and suggest creative improvements and better ways of working.
- Demonstrate tenacity to achieve results.

And at the next level:

- Maintain simultaneously a broad strategic perspective and awareness of the detail of a situation.
- Adapt plans quickly in response to emerging situations and changing environments.
- Take calculated risks to improve performance.
- Able to act decisively and quickly.

I suggested a fifth area too—*Motivating and influencing others*—and perhaps this is more the preserve of those involved in initiating or leading collaboration. The behaviors I'd expect to observe include being able to:

- Communicate humanitarian values and encourage others to share them.
- Inspire confidence in others.
- Speak out clearly for organizational beliefs and values.
- Demonstrate active listening to encourage team collaboration.
- Influence others positively to achieve program goals.

And going up a level toward mastery, the behaviors I'd expect to see those with substantial experience of working in collaboration or with partners include being able to:

- Inspire others by clearly articulating and demonstrating the values, core purpose and principles that underpin humanitarian work.
- Provide regular and ongoing informal and formal feedback.
- Recognize the contribution of others.
- Adapt leadership style to the time frame and changing situation.

Those competencies are drawn from work done with a consortium of humanitarian agencies, but I think they have stood the test of time and they provide a sound basis for drafting competencies for collaboration. A cross-check with the skills set out by the Partnership Brokers Association[4]

---

[4] http://partnershipbrokers.org/w/brokering/roles-and-skills/ (accessed April 1, 2015).

reveals strong alignment, although in my experience partnership brokers tend to require a greater level of competence in negotiation! I've included a brief summary (below) of what could be considered the core competencies for partnership, adapted from the Partnership Brokers Association's extensive materials:

Negotiation: helping partners differentiate between individual objectives and positions and negotiation based on meeting partners' underlying interests.

Synthesizing information and record keeping: able to manage and interpret complex data and layers of information and experience. Able to undertake or oversee accurate recording of meetings and decisions.

Communication and presentation: proficient in active listening, social interaction, empathy, concise speaking, presenting with impact and through stories and able to adapt communication for diverse audiences.

Coaching and capacity strengthening: able to support and coach partners in building their own brokering skills.

Institution building: understanding of governance and accountability procedures and able to support the partnership as it evolves and becomes more 'institutionalized'.

Reviewing and revising: facilitating—or overseeing the facilitation of— partnership reviews and the revision of partnership structure, processes and/or agreement.

Types of Collaborative Competencies

While my focus for the consortium was on core behaviors, other initiatives, such as the IBM Center for Business of Government in their guide to collaborative competencies,[5] have gone further and taken time to develop—and categorize—more detailed competencies specifically relating to collaboration. Again, I've included a brief summary of the

---

[5] http://www.businessofgovernment.org/blog/business-government/guide-collaborative-competencies (accessed April 1, 2015).

five categories they identified for reference, adapted from their extensive guide:

Leadership and management competencies, such as: planning, organizing and managing for collaboration; collaborative problem-solving and conflict resolution management skills.

Process competencies, such as: communicating effectively, including cross-cultural presentations and persuasion; working in teams and facilitating group decision-making; managing conflict constructively in groups.

Analytical competencies, such as: applying analytical skills and strategic thinking by understanding political, legal and regulatory contexts; developing measures of progress and assessing and evaluating performance of the group.

Knowledge management competencies, such as: integrating technical and scientific information for informed decision-making; using information technology to communicate and operate in social networks.

Professional competencies, such as: acting upon principles of fairness, transparency and inclusiveness; balancing personal, professional and institutional loyalties with the group's requirements for success.[6]

Collaborative Personalities?

There's not so much literature covering what constitutes a collaborative personality and whether certain personalities are more predisposed toward collaboration or not. But the blogosphere is alive with thinking and ideas. Our own work at The Conscious Project using psychometric instruments such as the Myers Briggs Type Indicator has shown us that the issue is a lot more nuanced than a simple extroversion/introversion trait. Clearly those whose energy is focused outwards may have a head start when it comes to initiating and/or developing a collaborative relationship and talking through ideas, but the reflective approach typical of introverts also has an essential role in a partnership. What we can say is that collaboration thrives when individuals have a high degree of emotional, cultural and

---

[6] Ibid.

social intelligence and are able to adapt their working style and recognize subtle differences in the working style of their colleagues, making appropriate adjustments, in the best interests of the collaboration.

Rather than holding to the view that only certain personalities can collaborate or that certain personalities have the advantage when it comes to collaboration, we'd do better to focus our energy on understanding each other better. If you're put off by some of the traditional psychometric tools then more accessible frameworks such as those featured on websites such as Lifehacker,[7] (for example the Big Five[8] personality traits), may be more helpful as a way of understanding people's personalities:

> *Extraversion*: How talkative, energetic, and assertive a person might be.
> *Agreeableness*: How sympathetic, kind or affectionate is this person?
> *Conscientiousness*: How organized and plan-oriented someone might be.
> *Neuroticism*: How tense or moody vs. emotionally stable is this person?
> *Openness to new ideas*: How imaginative, open-minded and insightful someone is.

What this reminds us is that self-awareness and awareness of others is critically important and that, along with our mindset, determines whether collaboration can take place, as well as its success.

The Importance of Feedback

Earlier in this chapter I identified giving feedback (specifically the ability to provide regular and ongoing formal and informal feedback) as a core behavior. There's no doubt at all in my mind that being able to give effective feedback is vitally important, yet sadly my experience is that feedback skills are severely lacking or underdeveloped among those working in the aid sector. That's beyond unfortunate! Unless we are able to master this skill then any collaboration we are involved in will be compromised, and

---

[7] http://lifehacker.com/how-to-read-your-coworkers-personalities-for-better-col-1700511598 (accessed October 1, 2015).

[8] S. Srivastava, (2015). *Measuring the Big Five Personality Factors*. Available at: http://psdlab.uoregon.edu/bigfive.html (accessed October 1, 2015).

for those of us in the aid sector, the costs of such a failure is high—and not just to us.

Feedback is challenging when given interculturally, and care should be taken when giving feedback in group settings, across wide age differentials, in hierarchical settings and between genders and different ethnic groups. But with practice and support, it is a skill that can be improved and the benefits reaped quickly. Given that there are plenty of resources on the web and widely available, I won't digress at length here, but there are two key points I want to make.

The first is that, as in a typical management situation, there are essentially two types of feedback we can give, and those working in a collaboration can benefit as much from these as an individual direct report. The two types of feedback are reinforcing feedback or redirecting feedback. When those involved in collaborative activity are encouraged and empowered to regularly give feedback, then the whole collaboration benefits, and this is true for feedback that reinforces or affirms the direction of travel, or discussions or behaviors. When those working in a collaboration feel that behavior is out of place or the direction of travel does not align with the agreed values or principles, or is unlikely to deliver the desired outcome, then redirecting feedback is called for.

Secondly, a framework for giving feedback can be very helpful. With due acknowledgment to the Center for Creative Leadership, with whom People In Aid partnered for several years, one of the most helpful techniques I've come across was developed by the Center for Creative Leadership and is known as the Situation, Behavior Impact model.[9] It's a simple technique for giving feedback and which I've found to work well in many different countries, throughout Central America, the USA, Africa, the Middle East, central, south and South-East Asia and Australia and the Pacific.

Situation
Situates feedback in time and place (location) so that the receiver can recall and understand the context.

---

[9] http://www.ccl.org and http://www.ccl.org/leadership/pdf/community/SBIJOBAID.pdf (both accessed October 1, 2015).

Behavior

The actions (words, behaviors) that were observed and allows the individual receiving feedback to know exactly what they did.

Impact

Feelings and thoughts the feedback giver had, and how the feedback giver (or others) behaved as a result of the receiver's behavior.

Collaborations thrive when communication and dialogue is honest, open and respectful, and effective collaboration depends on the gift of feedback. Collaborations benefit when communication is based on what a colleague in Oxfam once referred to as 'Full Frontal Frankness'. Such openness requires high levels of trust and a clear, unrelenting focus on the common goal which includes an agreement to hold one another accountable in the pursuit of that goal and the achievement of the desired outcome. I encourage all those I work with collaboratively to explore and define what such a level of communication means for them, and how they will ensure what needs to be said gets said.

Fig. 6.1 Feedback is a gift

In the early stages of a collaboration, it's not uncommon for the core team to invest in their personal intelligence by undergoing psychometric assessments and gathering 360° feedback to increase the understanding among team members and help create a high-performing team. I'd encourage this investment, as the more feedback we have on ourselves the more aware we become of how our actions and behaviors affect others, and what we can do to mitigate the negative impact and help create a positive collaborative environment.

In Summary

We've highlighted core collaborative behaviors such as active listening and the ability to give effective feedback. Developing collaborative competence is essential for all of us who work collaboratively, and that boils down to a small set of behaviors that we must develop and practice.

Although some personalities seem better suited to collaborating, I've suggested that everyone has the potential to collaborate provided they choose to model collaborative behaviors and remain open to collaboration.

For Reflection

As you think about being a conscious collaborator, why not take a few moments to reflect on:

- Whether you currently have what it takes to collaborate?
- Which competencies you need to focus on developing in order to collaborate more effectively?

7

'Generosity and Humility'

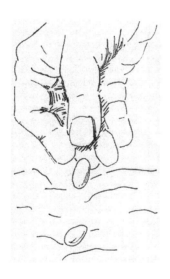

© The Editor(s) (if applicable) and The Author(s) 2016
B. Emmens, *Conscious Collaboration*,
DOI 10.1057/978-1-137-53805-5_7

Introduction

In this chapter we explore what I consider to be two of the most important values underpinning successful collaboration. They're not values that are talked about much today, and nor do they tend to feature prominently in corporate brochures, yet I can't think of a single successful collaboration where either or both of these values and their associated behaviors were not present in some form or another. They may seem out of place in our twenty-first-century thinking, but I believe we need to reclaim them, redefine them and reapply them. I realize I'm not the only voice saying this—in fact the volume is increasing and the number of books published within the last couple of years that touch on generosity and conscious business is testament to a growing interest in this area, and some dissatisfaction with the way business is being done.

We've seen that conscious collaboration requires authentic, honest relationships between individuals; and while we might not be at the stage of finding community in our collaborative endeavors, we do know that there are certain values that make for a healthy community. Generosity and humility being two of them.

Fundamentally, both generosity and humility have a great deal to do with power, and our individual attitudes toward power determine how we act or behave in a collaborative situation. Power can be quite hard to define—the *Oxford English Dictionary* says it like this:

> The capacity or ability to direct or influence the behaviour of others or the course of events.' Or 'Political or social authority or control,' or 'Authority that is given or delegated to a person or body.[1]

Power, particularly the imbalance of power, or the inappropriate exertion or influence of power, can have a huge bearing on the success of a collaboration and can impact individual relationships almost more than any other factor.

---

[1] http://www.oxforddictionaries.com/definition/english/power (accessed October 5, 2015).

Generosity

Let's begin by taking a closer look at generosity. It's no coincidence that one of the core values of The Conscious Project is generosity and this is how we describe it to clients and partners:

We think generously, listen generously, and live generously. Whether leading, doing or facilitating, our work is rooted in appreciative inquiry and positive psychology; we believe people realize their potential when they are inspired to be all they can be. We nurture a growth mindset in one another, and those we work with.[2]

Nature or Nurture?

I'm fascinated by how our notions of generosity are formed from an early age. I grew up in comfortable circumstances in the south-west of England; my family weren't rich (compared to many) but we were certainly not what I would call poor. We had a home and some land, I was well fed, I was educated, we took family holidays in the UK, my parents took an interest in what I was doing and supported me in various hobbies and pursuits. They were extremely generous with their time, to me and to all my siblings. But it went much further than that: it was a Christian home and my parents took their responsibility to be generous to others very seriously. I can't remember a week going by without them welcoming someone to our home, feeding them and generally showing kindness. They were generous with what they had and gave relentlessly. Sometimes as children we wondered why they did it, and I never really understood the answer—they seemed to have an unwavering belief that people had good in them, and would reciprocate generosity and kindness if ever they needed it. It sounded like an insurance policy, albeit with no guarantees, and an unpredictable premium! Yet mysteriously things did arrive in our lives. I'm sure as a result of my parents' generosity to others. An old car to

___
[2] http://www.theconsciousproject.org/what-we-do/ (accessed October 5, 2015).

learn to drive in, a laptop that was no longer quick enough for work but was fine for studying and writing essays.

Children are often renowned for their acts of kindness and generosity—it's as though their calculation is very straightforward. When they see someone who needs what they have (be it food or money or a toy) then they immediately work out how they can give what they have to solve the problem. At least that's mostly been my experience watching my own children. Naturally they also quickly identify the things they need which others have, and start plotting a way of obtaining them. But in general, most children I've spent time with—whether in my extended family, in schools, or in youth clubs—seem quick to show generosity. I wonder whether this is because if they give something, they are less worried about where they will get a replacement from, or perhaps it's because they question how can I help? or what can I do?, rather than calculating what's in it for them if they give.

This got me thinking—what if we applied this to the workplace? What if when we saw a need or new opportunity we took a moment to reflect on whether we could be a part of that, and whether we could contribute something from our own assets or resources? That would be a very different proposition from the typical 'what can I get from this situation?', or if I give something, 'how will I benefit?'. Much of the work I've done over the last few years has been in teams—collaborating to deliver a review or evaluation, or designing a process to achieve a desired goal—and one of the questions I've made a point of asking co-facilitators, as well as encouraging them to ask of one another is the very simple: 'How can I help you, right now?'. There are plenty of variations but taking time to reach out and discover the best thing we can do to help someone at any given moment is a powerful question and builds collaborative capital. The answer may be nothing at all, but more likely than not there is usually a straightforward task that can be done and this contributes to the building and strengthening of trust in the team.

How Much Does It Cost?

The issue with being generous is that it takes time; it's an investment of thinking and energy, and it requires us to give or release something which we may not want to let go of. This got me thinking further still—what can we give that costs us relatively little? What if we applied the principle of generosity to our thinking and to the words we use? Is it possible to become known for our generous thinking and our generous words? I think we might be onto something here. It might certainly reassure any investors or backers who are concerned about unbridled generosity with no guarantee of a fiscal return.

Thinking Generously

Often what we think remains hidden—we tuck it away in our consciousness and depending on various factors, including our cultural norms, we are very choosy about how and to whom that thinking is revealed. I believe 'thinking generously' is a discipline we can nurture, and it costs us very little. It's a discipline that is especially important in the context of collaboration and it entails us choosing a starting point where we assume the best and continue to assume the best until proven otherwise. By assume the best I mean we credit the individual or organization with whom we are collaborating to act out of honest intention or motive, unless we have very good evidence to suggest that is completely foolish, in which case there are bigger issues for the collaboration to address! Thinking generously means we resist being drawn into the cul-de-sac of cynicism in which we continually question motives or look for evidence that an action is not in the collaboration's best interest. Thinking generously permits us to objectively process information when we receive it and not look for hidden meanings or messages. Thinking generously discourages us from keeping a tally of rights and wrongs and working toward a day of reckoning, for which read 'almighty bust-up'. Thinking generously requires us to make judgments based on fact and behavior, not our prejudices and preconceptions.

Fig. 7.1   Working toward a day of reckoning

Generous Words

Our words tend to reflect what we think, though plenty of cultures have made an art form out of saying anything but what they think, or by using deliberately obtuse or euphemistic language to mask true sentiments. My non-British colleagues often poke fun at me for this, joking that the words I say are code for something quite different! It's true that the internet has plenty of examples of useful tables containing everyday British expressions along with a translation (aimed at non-Brits), but there's a serious point here. We can all choose to use clear, unambiguous language—but sometimes we don't.

Going further, there is also a serious point to be made about appreciation and affirmation in the context of collaboration. Generous words extend to acknowledgment when a team member has gone the extra mile, or put in special effort, and affirming participation is a necessary act when collaborating.

Dealing with Disappointment

If we accept that in a collaboration it is better to be judged as generous and gracious than mean-spirited, then sooner or later we will find ourselves in a dilemma. We may sense that we have been taken advantage of, or that our goodwill and generosity is being exploited. This is a real issue, and potentially a collaboration-breaker. How do we respond? How can we deal with such a disappointment?

I suggest that we set about the feedback process we looked at in Chap. 6 as we would for any other type of feedback, and take quick action. The most important thing is to establish the facts and determine whether there has been a misunderstanding, and whether for the sake of the collaboration the situation can be resolved and restored. It may not be possible of course, and occasionally such actions do lead to an irreversible breakdown of trust, but a salvage process should not be considered impossible until all avenues have been explored.

Thinking and speaking generously are intentional acts, just as collaboration is an intentional process. We can practice generosity, and get better at it!

Humility

Now let's take a look at humility. Arguably even less popular than generosity, humility tends to be associated with ancient prophets or gurus, and the preserve of certain leadership models which some faith-based INGOs have espoused (for example servant leadership). Attitudes differ around the world, but in the West humility does not generally seem to be a value or state that people aspire to. Certainly the initial reaction whenever I mention it is one of incredulity, bordering on disbelief. Am I some kind of religious nut? What on earth do I mean?

I think perhaps we've misunderstood humility though, and it's time to take a fresh look and see what it could mean for us in our organizations and particularly in our collaborations.

Genuine Humility

Humility is generally taken to mean 'having a modest or low view of one's importance,'[3] and this is a helpful starting point. In a collaboration the vision and outcome are the important driving forces. After that, it is the individuals that participate, what they bring and how they work together that really matters. When I say that humility is important, I don't mean the false modesty or tedious self-deprecation that is often confused with genuine humility and which can poison collaborative relationships. False modesty and self-deprecation can be passive-aggressive behaviors, or associated with the mantle of victimhood; they are to be avoided. What we should be striving for is a genuine understanding of our place in a collaboration and an acknowledgment of the collaborative capital that exists, for these are both prerequisites for successful collaboration.

In Service to?

Humility can also grow out of a deep recognition of what we are in service to. In the early days of The Conscious Project, I spent many hours with Rajan Rasaiah, who is a truly remarkable coach. He would often challenge me by saying, 'But Ben, what is this in service to?',[4] and then encourage me to describe the big vision and greater goals, and who we needed to work with to achieve them. At the same time his challenge was encouraging, in that it freed me to assume my place and role in the collaboration, and stop trying to be someone I wasn't, to solve everything or to do everything. A lack of humility can make us a prisoner of our own ambition—we can be desperately committed to a vision and outcome, and yet somehow

---

[3] http://www.oxforddictionaries.com/definition/english/humility (accessed October 5, 2015).
[4] Rajan Rasaiah, Verve and Values, in discussion with the author, August 2012.

blind to the need for others to play a role in achieving it and unable to comprehend the power of collaboration. And at the extreme end, a lack of humility can manifest as pride and arrogance, a toxic combination in any partnership and of no real value to a collaboration.

When Sara Swords and I were given an opportunity by Oxfam back in 2011 to build on the success of the core humanitarian competencies framework by leading the development of a core humanitarian skills development program and a management and leadership skills program, again for humanitarians, we were faced with a dilemma: there was no way we could do that ourselves in the time we had. To develop programs that would be welcomed by a wide range of humanitarian organizations we would firstly have to curate a huge amount of content that already existed, and then we would need to work with a much larger team to develop, test and refine the content and mode of delivery. And ultimately we knew that whatever we created would need to be constantly evolving and adapting to suit the local context. The end result would be a long way from the early pilot programs, and we would have to accept that having many different individuals get involved would be in the best interests of the project. We also had to accept that the nature of the funding also meant that whatever was produced would be open-source and available for anyone and any organization to use and adapt. We had to adopt an attitude of generosity and humility in order to ensure the work benefitted from our best thinking, and we and our learning and development colleagues would have to relinquish our desire for control and recognition. I remember explaining this approach at the time to Oxfam's project manager, Caroline Hotham, and the relief when I realized she had understood completely. There was never any question in her mind as to the ultimate project purpose and the desired outcome: it was to develop humanitarian competencies and equip technical and managerial staff with the skills to deliver outstanding emergency response programs that had disaster- and conflict-affected people at the center of all that we did. That was so helpful and freed us and everyone working on the development of the context programs to participate and contribute as equals.[5]

---

[5] http://www.contextproject.org (accessed October 5, 2015).

Rebalancing Power

In any collaboration, when we put to one side any preconceptions or ideas about how important or powerful we are, we play an important role in the rebalancing of power. Of course we may have valuable ideas and a tangible contribution to make, but the point is when we consider ours to be better ideas or a more important contribution than anyone else's, we slowly quench the collaborative spirit and trust begins to break down. I'm coming to the conclusion that a spirit of humility involves a conscious relinquishing of power. Not the discarding or jettisoning of power, but a releasing of our grip on power in order that the power that exists elsewhere in the room or in the collaboration has its voice and its moment to influence the direction.

At The Conscious Project, we've adopted humility as one of our core values. Here's what we say:

> We don't put ourselves on a pedestal or come with one-size-fits-all shiny solutions! We are human, and when it comes to society, we are part of the problem as well as part of the solution. Our work is not about 'us' as experts, or reinforcing inequality or vested interest; rather, it is gently disruptive, and about the 'collective us' and a connected world. We each have a part to play and our methodologies unlock your own expertise, insight and experience, so that together we can craft the best possible outcomes.[6]

Reading it back now, the term 'collective us' seems slightly odd! What did we mean? We wanted to reinforce the point that conscious collaboration creates outcomes that are in our collective best interest. That's in contrast to collaboration that serves only the interests of a small minority or an elite, which may be a conscious choice, but is simultaneously unconscious of the needs or interests of wider society.

Gentle Disruption

The other point I'd like to highlight is that in a culture of genuine humility, questions are permitted—even encouraged—and as we have seen, questions and constructive challenge are essential for a collaboration to thrive.

---

[6] http://www.theconsciousproject.org/what-we-do/ (accessed October 5, 2015).

That's what I mean by gentle disruption: not a noisy, aggressive questioning approach in which we show how clever we are, but rather respectful and incisive questions that constructively challenge, and momentarily disrupt thinking, leading to more questions that refine understanding, and a conscious re-engagement with the vision and clarification of the desired outcome. Duke Stump said it perfectly at the Do Lectures in 2013: 'We need to quiet our cleverness.'[7]

Finally, on humility, in the words of my co-director Abi:

> Humility is one of the foremost enablers. It allows another the floor, listens attentively while they speak their truths, and all the while, esteems. Humility is key to effective progress; when we are all tied up in 'me' and 'my idea' we sacrifice the greater benefits on the altar of self-absorption, and reject input that could provide development, extension and even transformation.[8]

Be on Your Guard

Collaboration can be built effectively where there is a spirit of generosity and humility, and when the outcome of the collaboration is for the greater good, then it is perhaps easier to act generously and with humility. We each have a responsibility to be intentional about the collaborative behaviors we choose, and we should recognize that when collaborating, certain behaviors are dangerous and risk derailing the collaboration. In particular we should guard against our competitive nature, and be aware when we are about to act out of selfishness or self-interest and when the words we choose might come across as proud or arrogant.

In Summary

In this chapter I've presented two core values which underpin collaboration—generosity and humility. Often misunderstood, they play an important role in creating a culture that is conducive for collaboration,

---

[7] Duke Stump at the Do Lectures in discussion with the author, April 2013. http://thedolectures. com (accessed October 5, 2015).

[8] Abi Green, The Conscious Project, essays and in discussion with the author, August 2014.

by encouraging open constructive questions—assuming collaborators have good intentions—and ensuring that the focus remains on the vision and outcomes and not personalities or positions.

Power, especially when unevenly distributed or inappropriately wielded, corrupts collaboration. Generosity and humility are values which—when genuinely present—force a rebalancing of power. If we are successful in cultivating the ability to think generously, then generous words will flow. When we each consider one another's views and opinions as more important, a mutually respectful culture grows and the result is that at its best, everyone's ideas and opinions have equal weight and equal airtime and can be robustly debated. Where there is generosity and humility even the quieter voices get the chance to be heard, and so trust grows and collaboration prospers.

For Reflection

As you think about the core values of generosity and humility, why not take a few moments to reflect on:

- How you act generously in your collaborations?
- Where can you identify new opportunities to demonstrate generosity?
- When have you demonstrated humility in the context of collaboration?
- What challenges you most when it comes to humility?

8

'Accompaniment'

'The path is made by walking.' (African proverb)

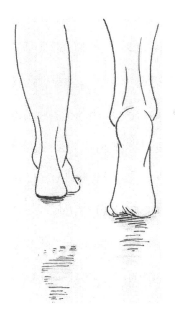

B. Emmens, *Conscious Collaboration*,
DOI 10.1057/978-1-137-53805-5_8

Introduction

This chapter explores 'accompaniment', both as a value and a behavior, and in particular how it relates to the facilitation and partnership brokering role. I've long felt it to be true that collaboration is about stepping out into uncharted territory, with unfamiliar topography and an absence of landmarks or familiar features that can reassure us along the way. Often all we have is a description of the destination, perhaps the coordinates, while in our hands is a compass and on our backs are some provisions.

But just as every journey begins with the first step, it's equally true that—just as the African proverb reminds us—'the path is made by walking'. True collaboration, especially that which sets out to solve an 'unsolvable' problem or a gigantic and complex challenge, requires us to create new paths. And for those of us who have a special role to play in terms of brokering and facilitating collaboration, we absolutely need to be prepared to get dusty feet.

To Accompany (Vb.)

The act of accompanying is a little lost in the Western world. It still applies in the context of unaccompanied minors (children) who travel alone, but other than that it's not a word we come across that often. Elsewhere, it has a kind of application in parts of the Middle East and Asia where unmarried women (in particular) are expected to be accompanied when outside the home. But that's always seemed closer to chaperoning in my view, and that is a much less helpful concept when we're thinking about collaboration.

One way in which the act of accompanying has been brought to life for me is through being a parent, and by benefitting from practical support, encouragement and wisdom from other parents as I've worked through new experiences. In truth I had no idea just how hard it would be, nor in fairness how much fun it would be, simultaneously, but like many things that are worth experiencing and that teach us so much about ourselves, it is at the same time exhausting and incredibly rewarding. The thing is, as clichéd as it sounds, a child does not come with an instruction manual, so you have to work stuff out and reach your own decisions and stand by them. The best hope you have is to connect with other parents who can reassure you that it was just the same for them, and if you're fortunate you will be able to benefit from their experience. If ever you talk to someone who has had a second or third child (or more), most will tell you (with a glint in their eye) that very little prepared them for the arrival of the second or third. Some learning was helpful of course, but techniques and approaches that worked first time round mysteriously stopped working with the second or third child. So yet again, the community of wisdom and support from other parents was needed. It's no coincidence that there's another African proverb that goes along the lines of 'it takes a village to raise a child'. I used to wonder what that meant, as though somehow parents were absolving themselves of their responsibility, but now I have a clearer sense of what it might mean. Parents will always be parents, but the complex task of raising a child requires many different inputs and—done well—is the result of conscious collaboration between parents, relatives, carers, friends, teachers, medical staff, coaches, mentors and more.

Pooled Resources

In conscious collaboration, relevant assets and resources are often pooled and it's the performance of the team that matters, much more than any one individual shining brightly. There are inherent risks of course in doing this—just as there are for any team that comes together to achieve a goal—the assets may be depleted or resources may run out; individuals may use more than their fair share; individuals may not pull their weight or take an equal share of the workload. It's true those are all real risks, and this highlights the importance of preparation and planning. Of course it's hard to know in advance what you'll need if the territory you're heading to is uncharted and you haven't been there before. A suitable response involves contingency planning and exploring a few possible scenarios.

One of the things I learnt by doing the Ten Tors Challenge was the importance of scrutineering! At 14 years of age, the notion of being scrutineered sounded most unpleasant, and I don't think any of my team knew what it meant, other than that all our kit would be unpacked and meticulously inspected by army officers and volunteers to ensure we were suitably prepared for various eventualities such as bad weather, accidents or injuries, and also that we had sufficient food, clothing and shelter. It was exactly that—and compliance with the event rules and regulations was in our best interest or we would be thrown out. And to keep us on our toes, the threat of spot-checks ensured no-one lightened their load by leaving out a crucial but heavy item.

Fast forward to three years later, and this time in the same team (but with a couple of new members), our approach to scrutineering was a little different. We were tackling the longest distance possible in the day-and-a-half event—55 miles—and weight mattered a whole lot more than it did when the distance was 35 or 45 miles. I remember us stretching every rule possible, but the scrutineering process remained the same—unpacking every item and letting it be inspected to ensure the team had left nothing out. What changed that time round though was the nature of the team's approach—it was much less a case of everyone taking along duplicate kit just in case, and instead our priority was first to work out which kit was needed, then to lay it out to determine which was lightest and most compact, and only then did we divide it equally among us. The same went for food and emergency supplies. Personal items were kept to an absolute minimum and usually involved some customization—I even have a surreal memory of sawing the handle off my toothbrush to save a few grams! The different, pooled approach saved close to 10kg per person in terms of what we had to carry in our backpacks—most welcome!

In my experience many collaborative efforts also begin with a lot of duplication. People bring with them similar resources, just in case, and the frank discussion about what is actually required, whether in terms of physical resources or technical skills and capacities, doesn't happen until some time down the line. This is especially true when a collaboration comes together in order to achieve a goal, and less so for an existing team that decides it will collaborate on something new. We could often save ourselves a lot of wasted time and effort by pooling the resources and sharing the load. Walking side by side is a powerful metaphor for collaboration, and conscious collaboration at its best evokes a strong sense of community, characterized by mutual support and accompaniment.

The Fifth Rider

Some cycling races still feature a team time trial, a race against the clock where the sole aim is for the team to cover the allotted distance in the shortest possible time. In the team time trial, however, it's not the time of the first rider across the line which counts—it's that of the fifth rider. Some teams choose to get the maximum possible from the sixth, seventh, eighth and ninth riders (assuming none have dropped out of the race prior to that point and they are all able to start) and once those riders have given their all they are then 'dropped' (left behind), while other teams choose to share the work as a team of nine right until the final sprint for the line. Spectators will often see a team regrouping and nursing their slower riders along before the strongest five make one last push for the line. Whichever tactics are chosen, the team time trial gives a unique insight into how cyclists have to adapt to the situation and context, as well as provide mutual support. I guess it's not quite accompaniment in the strictest definition but there is something inspiring about watching a team ease off slightly (or even wait) for their fifth rider, and then stick with them, encouraging them and getting them over the line so the clock can be stopped. As a metaphor, it's one that challenges us to reflect on how we might need to bring accompaniment to life while working in a collaboration. As with my Ten Tors Challenge all those years ago, we simply don't know at what point we might need to ease the pace for someone in our partnership or collaboration, or who will need to be supported (or carried). It happens more often than we think, and we should be prepared for such an eventuality.

Active Listening

In Chap. 6 we highlighted active listening as a core behavior for collaboration, and I would say unequivocally that it's one of the most important features of accompaniment. Accompanying someone not only means coming alongside and journeying together, it means actively listening to what they have to say and asking questions that unlock new thinking. It means taking a few moments to check in when you meet or connect, or taking a few moments out and sitting down together, or sharing a coffee (or cup of tea) or going for a walk. In other words it entails being together, and becoming a 'thinking partner'—someone who helps others think and talk things through, someone who is able to challenge but doesn't pass judgment. It entails playing the role of critical friend. Collaboration thrives when we understand the value of accompaniment and practice it.

In his writing about the principles of empathetic communication,[1] Stephen Covey talks about the importance of seeking first to understand, and highlights the danger of listening with the intent to reply. Listening with the intent to reply is something we're all guilty of at some point or another—it takes tremendous self-discipline not to, especially when ideas are flowing fast or deadlines are approaching. However, collaboration can be more fruitful when listening is prioritized, and given space and time. As a facilitator of collaborative teams, I often find myself asking more vocal individuals to hold back in order that we hear the quieter voices, and in the same way that we might read between the lines to detect nuance and deeper meaning, I think it's important that we cultivate the discipline of 'listening between the lines' and avoid filling every gap in conversation or silent moment.

Shared Experiences

A shared experience counts for a lot on the collaboration journey. Through moments of darkness as well as the brighter times, we grow: learning happens and bonds are forged. An invitation to 'accompany' is more easily extended to those who have some prior experience that we see as credible or valuable, and that we can benefit from, than it is to those who will require a great deal of emotional investment. After all, it's no fun journeying with someone who we consider to be high maintenance. However, paradoxically, significant learning can be gained when those in a partnership or collaboration are all starting from a similar position (whether knowledge or ignorance). Stepping out into the unknown with

---

[1] Stephen R. Covey, *The 7 Habits of Highly Effective People*, London, Simon & Schuster, 1989, pp. 239–241.

someone alongside us somehow isn't as daunting as going solo, even if the person accompanying us has no direct experience of what lies ahead either.

A few years ago, when I was a Director at People In Aid, I and my counterpart at the Headington Institute,[2] Lisa McKay, decided we really should collaborate and develop some joint programs. We had similar views on resilience and were both working on stress and trauma issues within the aid sector. We had met each other a few times and got on very well, and we were excited at the prospect of working together. We were both given freedom by our respective bosses to develop some proposals and after a number of successful events in the US and the UK, we found ourselves in Indonesia running a two-day workshop on stress and resilience for aid workers. We'd allocated time to draft a collaboration agreement and had taken care of most of the logistics; lots of planning calls had taken place, and so we arrived in Jakarta the day before the workshop began. Lisa had flown in from Los Angeles and I had come in from London. I had instructions on how to get to a spacious and serviced apartment that Lisa had negotiated from some family friends (she had visited Jakarta often before), but it wasn't until I was sitting in the legendary Jakarta traffic that a number of things dawned on me... one was that although we'd worked together on various events, and produced various joint publications, we hadn't actually co-facilitated; the second was that although I'd worked in southern Asia I hadn't actually been to Indonesia before, and third was that although Lisa had managed to negotiate a workshop venue, generously provided by the Jakarta International Christian Fellowship, we had no host agency in-country to support us with logistics. Consequently, the day before the workshop would need to be spent setting up, sorting photocopies, collating participant packs and so forth. I was pretty stressed as I sat in that car heading toward the apartment, not really knowing what to expect, nor how the next few days would turn out. Lisa's experience of Jakarta would turn out to be invaluable.

As soon as I called up to the apartment and Lisa answered, I had a sense things would work out—she had already slotted back into Jakarta

---

[2] http://www.headington-institute.org (accessed October 1, 2015).

life and was recognizing landmarks from previous visits and even some of the local language, Bahasa Indonesia. We didn't really know what lay ahead, but as we sat down and worked out the schedule for the following day, and what needed to be done, things began to fall into place. It dawned on me that we were both stepping into the unknown, but the fact we were doing it together somehow made it much less overwhelming. Even when the only copier we could find was in the store room of a stationery shop in the basement of a nearby mall, and needed unjamming after every ten copies, even when the catering didn't quite work out, we accompanied one another and managed to deliver a workshop that the participants enjoyed and benefitted from a great deal.

Looking back I can see that stepping out into the unknown, taking some risks and extending ourselves beyond our comfort zones strengthened our collaboration. The shared experience, stories and understanding meant that although we didn't get an opportunity to do more workshops we did collaborate on a number of other projects in the years subsequently, and remain in contact as close friends.

The Jakarta experience and collaborating with Lisa taught me a lot; her great sense of humor kept me smiling through some pretty stressful moments, and her extensive networks meant that she was able to draw down on her social capital. In turn we were able to run a great workshop. I've worked in Indonesia many times since, and each time I arrive in Jakarta I recall my first visit—I remember the queasy feeling of not knowing what lay ahead and the way in which I was accompanied by Lisa. As a result, on occasions when I've traveled with a colleague who is working in a particular country for the first time, I've been able to offer reassurance and play the role of accompanier.

Always Be Learning!

In all aspects of life, being open to learning, whether opportunities present themselves or not, is vital. Being able to 'learn as you go', and then make adjustments or course-corrections, is a particularly useful skill when collaborating. But it is a rare skill and despite the noise organizations make about their commitment to learning, the rhetoric often masks the reality. Being able to learn in real time requires space to do so, and confident, competent individuals who are prepared to regularly ask questions that unlock insight and learning. In organizational environments or cultures where permission tends to be required before anything out of the ordinary is done, learning is often relegated to an agenda item in progress update meetings, or to the end of year/end of project reviews. The aid sector is notorious for is notorious for this despite having whole departments that are dedicated to monitoring, evaluation and learning. This makes for INGOs that have become very good at identifying lessons, but it is sometimes hard to tell whether an organization is actually *learning* from its experience.

I've spent a long time working with and supporting collaborations over the years—long enough to have seen a fair few learning initiatives come and go, and certainly long enough to see the same mistakes repeated. I wonder whether we're making things too complicated when it comes to learning? With the myriad mechanisms for monitoring and evaluation I fear we may have somehow lost sight of the crucial issue of personal responsibility and accountability.

For organizations to learn, teams need to learn, and for teams to learn, individuals need to learn. The same is true for collaborations—for the collaboration to learn the partners in the collaboration need to learn, and that in turn means that the individuals themselves need to be open to learning. One way in which individuals can help nurture a learning environment in a collaboration is by getting into the habit of asking a couple of simple, tried and tested questions at regular intervals. We can each take responsibility for asking questions, and listening to the response. For me it boils down to these two simple questions:

* What went well?
* What would you do differently next time?

If we asked nothing else, these two questions alone create huge opportunities for reflection, learning and change. Over the last 15 years I've worked in close to 40 countries around the world and I've used these questions in pretty much every single one of them. They cut through cultural inhibitions and work across ethnicities, ages and gender. These questions open the way for powerful learning moments. I would strongly advocate the principle of 'learner goes first', that is to say we hold back until an individual or individuals have spoken. Try it and I'm certain you will begin to see the benefits in terms of strengthened trust, more open communication and feedback and improved performance.

There's robust research to support using the appreciative approach (google 'research relating to appreciative inquiry' and 'appreciative dialogue' if you're skeptical). And there's robust research to support the use of these two questions which were born out of the research of author David Pendleton[3] (and others) into the doctor–patient interaction and the way learning happens in the medical profession. Pendleton found that in order to achieve the best learning and performance improvements in medical contexts, and to avoid mistakes being covered up or blame being apportioned, doctors were typically more open and honest and likely to improve performance when an appreciative approach was chosen over traditional performance reviews whose emphasis was on compliance and zero tolerance (of mistakes).

How the Conscious Project Does Accompaniment...

Accompaniment is one of the four core values at the Conscious Project—this is how we introduce it:

> Our approach is to come alongside you, whether virtually or in person, and to join you on your journey. We will listen to your story, and by turn we will play the role of 'critical friend', encourager, coach and thinking partner. Our style of coaching is solutions focused, again, anchored in an appreciative approach that enables you to draw on your strengths and experience.[4]

---

[3] David Pendleton, *The Consultation: An Approach to Learning and Teaching*, Oxford, Oxford University Press, 1984. Republished as *The New Consultation: Developing Doctor–Patient Communication*, Oxford, Oxford University Press, 2003. See also http://ukcatalogue.oup.com/product/9780192632883.do and http://patient.info/doctor/consultation-analysis (accessed October 1, 2015).

[4] http://www.theconsciousproject.org/what-we-do/ (accessed July 1, 2015).

When I asked my co-director Abi Green to describe it, she put it like this:

> Perhaps one of the most important reassurances is this: You are not alone! While solitude can be profoundly supportive to our growth and self-awareness, plain loneliness has undertones of sadness and fear. Accompaniment is the quiet partner who walks alongside you, listening both to the silence and the thoughts that are voiced. Accompaniment embodies the principle of empathy. It is the travelling partner who takes your hand when you take the deep breath to jump, releasing it in time to call out 'Fly!'[5]

But what does it really mean? What does it practically translate to?

It's an important question. One of our guiding principles when accepting work that generates revenue is that it is conscious work, that is to say we need to be convinced the client is prepared to be conscious and engage with difficult questions or issues, and that they are open to learning. It means that whenever we work, and especially when management consulting, facilitating and developing leadership programs, we actively seek ways of transferring knowledge and skills to our client. It means we take time to identify the competencies which could be developed during the work, and that we work hard to integrate a capacity-strengthening element with the actual delivery of the work.

In reality, we strive to work in partnership and collaboratively whenever we can. We make that a criteria for choosing who to work with and for the type of work we undertake. Of course, we accept that a collaboration or partnership won't always be possible, and we accept that although it may be a part of a conscious process—for example clinical mentoring and supervision or facilitating an action learning set—the contract itself will be a transaction. And that's fine—a contract for services has its place!

We know that we can bring our best selves and do our best work when we accompany, and when the collaboration is a partnership in which we can generously share what we have learnt, reinvesting social capital, and leaving an organization and its people in a much stronger position than when we joined. It makes for more fun and more memorable experiences, and we benefit too.

---

[5] Abi Green, The Conscious Project, essays and in discussion with the author, December 2014.

Mutual Responsibilities

One thing we've been reminded of in this chapter, yet again, is the importance of effective feedback. In a partnership and particularly when collaborating, each party is responsible for giving feedback effectively and regularly. Sometimes giving feedback is harder when you're close to someone or accompanying them, but over time and with practice many people find it becomes easier. That's another reason to prioritize accompaniment as a value—being alongside gives you an opportunity to notice small details and ask small questions along the way, rather than parachuting in the moment there is a crisis or a breakdown in communication. We owe this to each other—partnerships that are clear about the mutual accountability and are able to handle feedback and deal with issues quickly and appropriately become more resilient and more likely to achieve their goals.

In Summary

Accompaniment is in essence what conscious collaboration is all about—agreeing to journey together, in partnership, toward a common goal. Accompaniment is about being a critical friend as well as a thinking partner. Partnerships and collaboration rely on clear mutual accountability: we each have a responsibility to constructively challenge one another, and to give meaningful feedback that enables continuous learning. In a conscious collaboration it is by accompanying that we are able to collect feedback systematically swiftly act on it.

For Reflection

As you think about accompaniment, why not take a few moments to reflect:

- Who are your fellow travelers?
- Which partnerships give you an opportunity to 'accompany' and get dusty feet?

9

'The Edge of the Inside'

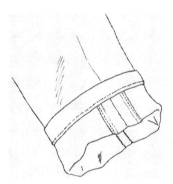

Introduction

Thinking about *where* collaboration happens is fascinating—to me at least! This chapter and Chap. 10 explore where effective and success-ful collaboration happens, and also looks at issues relating to risk, risk

© The Editor(s) (if applicable) and The Author(s) 2016
B. Emmens, *Conscious Collaboration*,
DOI 10.1057/978-1-137-53805-5_9

appetite and risk tolerance. One thing I've observed over the years is that conscious collaborators often operate around what I would term the edge of the inside, that is to say they remain within certain organizational parameters and rules, but sail as close to the limit (or edge) as they can in order to develop new products, services or relationships.

Looking back through history and where discoveries, developments or breakthroughs have been achieved—for example in science, exploration, engineering—we can see that innovation and the pioneering spirit tends to thrive at the edges. It's typically those who push the limits, who take things apart or who modify what exists that are able to come up with something new. In fact the more we look at this, the more we see it's true for almost every aspect of life, from farming and agriculture to the development of personal and mobile computing devices.

'Mind the Gap'

Our relationship with edges or boundaries is complex—many of us might recall being told as children to stay away from a glass pane, or from a cliff, or a river bank, or the edge of the sidewalk or platform… And there was good reason—being near the edge usually involves some degree of risk or danger, which those who were looking after us wanted to mitigate or eliminate.

But edges are a fact of life—some are clearly indicated, others less so—and they are a source of fascination. And human nature being what it is, we often have to go right to the edge to see what lies beyond and how we might get across the gap. We have to test those boundaries, those limits. For the most part that entails working right up to the edge, and depending on how rule-conscious we are and how scary the outside is, most people prefer to remain on the inside.

When children play we can observe that some are very curious indeed, always pushing toward the edge, exploring and experimenting, while others choose to stay in safety. One of the responsibilities of a parent is to ensure that learning space is safe and can withstand the pushing, and that the absolute boundaries are clear.

The Selvedge Edge

Edges or boundaries take a variety of forms, and some can be much stronger than others. Fabric aficionados will be familiar with the term 'selvedge'—it's the woven or sealed edge of fabric which holds the cloth on the loom and keeps the cloth from fraying or unraveling, and it entails a particular sort of weaving. For denim aficionados it is considered a thing of beauty and a sign of quality—selvedge denim often has more character (due to the slight irregularities that arise during the shuttle-weaving process which is much slower than typical mass-production looms) and the slow, steady weaving process produces less stress on the yarn, which ultimately makes the edge of the finished fabric more durable.

The story of selvedge reminds me that strong edges can be incredibly important: in textiles we usually don't want the edge to fray or unravel as it weakens the finished item. The same is true for collaboration—there is often a clear point of interface or connection, where one thing ends or becomes another thing. Care needs to be taken when joining two edges as seams are often a point of weakness in a garment and we can apply this metaphor to the seams that exist in an organization or collaboration—it's not a coincidence that the uneven selvedge edge is often unused or discarded when fabrics need to be joined. But by the same measure, an edge can be an important thing in its own right and sometimes there is no compelling case for collaboration: taking the selvedge denim analogy, we need to keep the selvedge edge intact and be able to work right up to our own boundary, relying on the strong systems and procedures (the woven fabric) and knowing that the rest of the organization can comfortably withstand the stress of our pushing to the limits.

'Edgelands'

Back in 2002 the British writer and environmentalist Marion Shoard[1] coined the term 'edgelands' as a way of describing the transitional, liminal areas of space typically found on the boundaries of country and

---

[1] http://www.marionshoard.co.uk and https://en.wikipedia.org/wiki/Edgelands (both accessed October 15, 2015).

town.[2] It struck me recently that I actually live in the edgelands—literally as well as metaphorically. My home is in North London and I have often described it to people as being 'where the grey hits the green'; although it's technically Greater London and an urban area, I am surrounded by trees, and a few minutes' walk from extensive green space and woodland. I live just inside the famous orbital motorway (the M25) that encircles the London area, although there are many bridges and underpasses which make crossing to the other side very easy.

I love the concept of edgelands and all that it conveys—and I am indebted to my friend, Ian Gee,[3] for bringing it to my attention. As an organization development specialist, Ian applies this concept to organizations and uses the term to perfectly describe the unnoticed and forgotten spaces in organizations where there is a different kind of freedom; he takes the view that all organizations have their edgelands—places where people work differently, often outside of organizational norms.

I believe that the edgelands are where some of the most exciting collaboration begins. In this chapter we'll take the view from the inside, and Chap. 10 will consider the view from the outside.

'The Edge of the Inside'

Many of the organizations I've worked with over the last decade are long established institutions and they have been fairly conservative (small 'c') in their collaboration practices. That is not to say they haven't been open to collaboration—quite the opposite in fact. They have loudly communicated the importance of partnerships, or collaborating, and they have sought out partnerships in order to do their work. Yet many partnerships have not lived up to the high expectations of either party, and there is plenty of research that suggests the aid sector still has a very long way to go in terms of establishing genuine partnerships that are truly collaborative, that is to say equitable and balanced, and respectful.

---

[2] http://www.marionshoard.co.uk/Documents/Articles/Environment/Edgelands-Remaking-the-Landscape.pdf (accessed October 15, 2015).

[3] http://edgelandsconsultancy.com (accessed October 15, 2015).

Many of the so-called partnerships I've been asked to evaluate reflect an imbalance in power and have more in common with client/contractor/sub-contractor relationships based around service agreements.

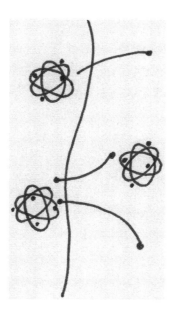

Fig. 9.1 The edge of the inside

One reason for this is because large aid organizations can be risk averse, and they can have cumbersome administrative and due diligence procedures. Aid workers will tell stories of how they managed to achieve a breakthrough or beat the system, and they usually involve phrases such as 'flying under the radar', or 'by stealth'. The further away individuals and operations are from head office oversight or controls, the more likelihood there is of being able to work a little more flexibly, contextually and freely. And some more decentralized organizations recognize this and openly encourage a decentralized power and decision making process whereby those closest to the aid recipients (and therefore closest to the organizational boundaries) have authority to make decisions.

Some of the more interesting collaborative initiatives I have been fortunate enough to be involved in within the aid sector have originated from humanitarian departments and emergency response teams. And this isn't surprising given the fact that in an organization, it is often the emergency responders who are able to raise funds quickly, are agile and quick to mobilize, quick to recognize opportunities and most likely to need to bend or stretch organizational rules in order to save lives. In some organizations it is this department or team that are seen as being on the cutting edge, or in my words, I would say that they are ones that are right at the edge of the inside, and well placed for any collaborative endeavor.

I'm a big fan of Kickstarter-type projects and a couple of years ago I helped crowd-fund a book that was being written by Liam Barrington-Bush called *Anarchists in the Boardroom*.[4] I was intrigued by the thought of drawing inspiration and learning from new forms of collective action and wanted to find out more… It's a good read with lots of ideas, some untested, and lots of questions, some unanswered. One of most interesting (and challenging) things about the book is the way it wrestles with the issue of change and how it happens. Like you I'm sure, I've seen plenty of examples where change happens from the inside, and plenty of examples where change has been catalyzed by external factors. And more often than not change results from both internal and external forces combining. I suggest that the same is true when it comes to collaboration: it is internal voices—stakeholders—that are often best placed to see opportunities. They have the vantage point which enables them to see the lie of the land, and toward the horizon, and with their insider-knowledge they have a good understanding of what type of collaboration will work well for their organization. And in terms of the external factors, it is often those on the edge of the inside of another organization that likewise see an opportunity and reach out.

The Humanitarian Leadership Academy

The closer we look, the more we see examples of collaboration emerging from the edge of the inside. One such example is the Humanitarian Leadership Academy[5] that was launched in March 2015 following

---

[4] http://morelikepeople.org/the-book/ (accessed October 15, 2015).
[5] http://www.humanitarianleadershipacademy.org (accessed October 15, 2015).

several years of detailed research into learning and professionalization within the aid sector. Initially hosted by Save the Children UK, and now fully-fledged and independent, at its heart is collaboration and a collaborative model. For several years senior staff within Save the Children's Emergencies department had been participating in sector-wide discussions about humanitarian learning and the department was renowned for initiating collaborative ventures with other INGOs and organizations.

Collaboration forms the backbone of the Humanitarian Leadership Academy's strategy to reach more than 100,000 people in over 50 countries over the next 4–5 years; as they say in their promotional literature:

> Collaboration is at the heart of meeting a challenge on this scale. We will partner with and draw on the experience of the corporate sector, learning professionals, academia, international institutions and NGOs from across the globe.[6]

Ambitious initiatives such as the Humanitarian Leadership Academy are certainly what are required to tackle the scale of the problems that exist. And bold ideas often come from visionaries who are in the system or in an organization and who see the consequences of inaction or insufficient response at first hand.

The Start Network

Other collaborative initiatives such as the Start Network,[7] which began life back in 2010 as the Consortium of British Humanitarian Agencies, have similar beginnings. A small number of Humanitarian Directors from different aid agencies, in many ways working at 'the edge of the inside', chose to meet to explore issues of common interest, each bringing their own perspective and with certain organizational standpoints.[8] From

---

[6] http://www.humanitarianleadershipacademy.org/wp-content/uploads/2013/10/Academy-4-Pager-August-2015.pdf (accessed October 15, 2015).

[7] http://www.start-network.org (accessed October 15, 2015).

[8] http://partnershipbrokers.org/w/wp-content/uploads/2010/08/Consortium-building-story-START-Network-July-2013-web.pdf (accessed October 15, 2015).

what the directors colloquially referred to as 'useful gatherings',[9] a more structured approach evolved with more formal frameworks and governance mechanisms, and in 2014 the decision was taken to 'uncouple' the Start Network from its host agency, Save the Children, and for it to become a new independent entity.

It is typically individuals working at the edge of the inside that we have to thank for ground-breaking initiatives such as the Start Network that demonstrate successful collaboration. All collaborations have their ups and downs, and there are twists and turns to navigate, and practical concerns which cause pressure and stress. Junction moments such as funding applications, receiving a large injection of funding or broadening the scope of activity can each place a collaboration under extreme pressure. But success at those moments is largely due to individuals with sufficient social capital and political acumen choosing to 'dig deep' into their reserves of stamina and strength in the interests of the collaboration.

Connectors

Thinking about community groups that I have worked with in the UK, as well as in Central America, sub-Saharan Africa and southern Asia, there are a number of common themes when it comes to a readiness to collaborate. One of those themes is that collaboration is often made possible as a result of the work of a 'connector' inside the organization, working tirelessly to present the case for collaboration, influencing the reform of policies and sometimes processes that will support collaboration, and then reaching out to connect with an external partner. We'll come back to this important point in Chap. 14, as the ability to connect is an important attribute and competence. But here, I'd like to link this concept of being a 'connector' to that of social capital which we considered in Chap. 5. Ultimately anyone can be a connector, and initiate a conversation about collaboration and collaborative possibility. In my experience connectors often gravitate toward the edge of an organization, not with the intention of leaving but because they naturally seek out connections wherever they

---

[9] Ibid., p. 2.

may be. Today the ability to connect is made easier through social media and an openness to connect seems to be an indicator of a more collaborative culture, or at least an openness to collaborate.

Remapping and Renegotiating the Edge

Much like the colonial borders of old, I think many of our traditional notions of boundary and border need to be challenged. The aid agencies I work with today increasingly find themselves under pressure to decentralize and, moreover, safety and security concerns mean that many have to work with remote partner organizations. Work that aid agencies traditionally undertook themselves is now done with, through or by partner agencies, and as some aspects of work become more specialist and technical, some organizations have made acquisitions or merged, while others have scaled up or down or redefined what it is they do.

This is an important aspect of collaboration—for at some point work done collaboratively may require underpinning structures or resources and it may make most sense to formalize a collaborative venture into a new operation. The edge of the inside becomes remapped and what is core gets redefined. In simple terms, at some point those at the edge of the inside may find themselves on the outside, whether that might be because they overstepped the mark or because the edge simply got redrawn.

Collaboration takes courage, and sometimes an extraordinary amount of courage. As Matthew Carter of CAFOD put in when referring to the early days of the Consortium of British Humanitarian Agencies: 'to be successful we had to be courageous enough to go into the unknown.'[10] And that is one of the hallmarks of conscious collaboration, an honesty that acknowledges the enormity of the challenge but trusts in the unity of purpose and is prepared to work for in the collective interest, despite considerable pressure to protect individual organizational interests.

---

[10] Ibid., p. 3.

In Summary

Conscious collaboration often begins at the edge of the inside, where connectors have a good vantage point of both what lies on the outside and toward the horizon, as well as having valuable insider knowledge which they can use to influence change, get buy-in and navigate political positions. From the inside, individuals often have a clear sense of what is frustrating the organization in achieving its vision, and depending on how far away they are from the vested power structures and controls, they may have sufficient autonomy to initiate conversations that may lead to collaboration, or to establish new connections.

However, edges have their place, and it can be in an organization's best interest to have a strong (selvedge) edge which enables individuals to work right up to the boundary without being worried that they will stress or break their organization or the system they are in.

'Edgelands' is another way of describing the edge of the inside and it is in the liminal spaces where freedom to collaborate is often greatest, perhaps because there is less scrutiny or maybe because there are fewer organizational norms to govern behavior and practice.

For Reflection

As you think about the being on the inside, looking over the edge toward the outside, why not take a few moments to reflect:

- How do you approach boundaries?
- In which direction are you instinctively likely to reach?
- How comfortable are you with operating at the edge of the inside?
- What opportunities do you have to be a 'connector'?

10

'The Porous Edge'

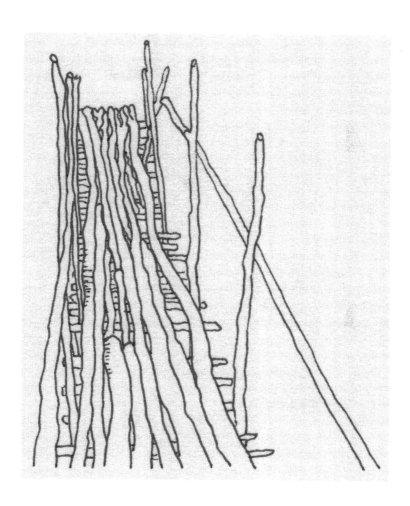

B. Emmens, *Conscious Collaboration*,
DOI 10.1057/978-1-137-53805-5_10

Introduction

Building on the topics covered in Chap. 9, this chapter develops the concept of 'edge', and explores what happens when conscious collaborators move beyond the edge and span boundaries.

We ended Chap. 9 by reflecting on opportunities we might have to be 'connectors', and by noting that conscious collaboration demands courage, often requiring conscious collaborators to extend themselves and move substantially outside of their comfort zone.

Boundaries...

We each approach boundaries differently, with different emotions and different strategies depending on how we've been brought up, how we've developed and crucially, how we approach risk. I wouldn't say I was an unbridled risk-taker, but a quick look from the outside might suggest otherwise: a racing cyclist and competitive mountain biker, a motorcyclist, a mountaineer, a traveler, an explorer, an aid worker, an entrepreneur... these are just labels, but they do perhaps indicate an adventurous spirit and suggest I have spent some time pushing boundaries, and occasionally overstepping them.

I wouldn't call myself a rule-breaker either, though I have a deep dislike of excessive bureaucracy and rules created to protect interests rather than help achieve a goal. As an HR professional much of my time was spent with leaders and managers doing my best to figure out how we could work within the spirit of the law rather than to the letter of the law, and act according to the collective best interest.

Porosity

When I was about 14 years old and falling in love with the great outdoors, I discovered an amazing fabric technology—GORE-TEX®.[1] It meant that when I wore a coat I could run about in the rain all day

---

[1] GORE-TEX® is a trade mark of W. L. Gore & Associates—http://www.gore-tex.co.uk/en-gb/home (accessed October 12, 2015).

and despite generating an unfeasible amount of heat (and therefore sweat) I could stay completely dry. It was miraculous—I'd read about it, then worked hard and saved my money so I could buy one. My parents were unconvinced—it wasn't cheap, and it seemed gimmicky. But it was a revelation—it was as though my body could breathe through the fabric and the evaporating moisture was able to escape through the GORE-TEX® membrane! Up until that point I'd only ever worn coats that were waterproofed in such a way that although rain didn't get in, heat and moisture vapor couldn't escape and therefore after a short while I would be soaked by my own perspiration. I can tell you it was as gross as it sounds, and risky too, because wet fabrics conduct heat much more quickly than dry fabrics and on the hills or in the mountains, that means exposure and a risk of hypothermia!

But there's a serious point here—and it's bound up with this notion of a porous membrane. I think some edges or boundaries can be porous—maybe more porous than we think—and that prompts a question: what if we saw the boundary or edge as porous, one that enabled us to pass though without too much hindrance, and connect in a new space? It seems to me that this takes us to a place where opportunities for collaboration could be plentiful.

The Porous Edge

When we spend stimulating time in the company of great thinkers, our thinking is often stretched beyond the normal limits. We are exposed to new ideas and ways of working which may be impossible for our organization to adopt. But it is a creative space, and one that can seed all sorts of opportunities for collaboration.

For those of us who consider ourselves to be pioneers—living and working at the 'edge of the inside' and forging new collaborative ventures—the notion of a 'porous' edge can make a great deal of sense as we move in and out of role. In my experience the porous edge is often the place where we see innovation, and where there is exhilaration.

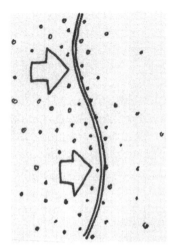

Fig. 10.1   The porous edge

Boundary Spanning

Another way of describing the porous edge is the term 'boundary span-ning,'[2] coined by colleagues at the Center for Creative Leadership. It was a real pleasure to collaborate with them during my time as a Director at People In Aid, and I learned a huge amount about leadership from them. I'm particularly indebted to Chris Ernst, co-author of the book *Boundary Spanning Leadership*,[3] and Steadman Harrison who took time to explain to me and a roomful of humanitarian leaders what boundary spanning leadership entailed. It's one of the most relevant concepts I've come across regarding collaboration, and well worth a read. Two of the six practices Chris Ernst and his co-author Donna Chrobot-Mason identified as being central to boundary spanning leadership were buffering and weaving,

---

[2] http://www.ccl.org/Leadership/landing/spanboundaries.aspx (accessed October 12, 2015).
[3] Ibid.

and while I can in no way do justice to their excellent book, I would like to highlight these two practices and explain briefly what they mean,[4] and how they are relevant to conscious collaboration.

Buffering

'Buffering is a way to monitor and manage the boundaries between groups.'[5] It creates inter-group safety by monitoring and protecting the flow of information and resources across groups. In many ways a buffer acts as a kind of filter, sifting out that which will distract a team or compromise the quality of the team's thinking.

One of the most important things the act of buffering achieves is to reduce the threat from external sources. Even when the threat is not an attack, the feeling of being threatened can easily arise in organizations or contexts where there is a lot of organizational change and feelings of insecurity among staff. The act of buffering helps individuals see how their identity and roles are evolving during a time of change; it can help reduce the threat from external influences and helps groups feel safe.

Sometimes, as we discussed in Chap. 9, boundaries have to be clear and visible, and the act of buffering creates space for staff to find their voice and speak out. It also helps in clarifying boundaries for other stakeholders.

The ability of leaders to act as a 'buffer' and shield their teams is an important competence, and in the context of collaboration, leaders who are able to buffer effectively often find that they have given space to the team members to collaborate more effectively, or to explore and initiate collaborative conversations that could ultimately lead to a partnership and working collaboratively. 'Buffering' requires social intelligence and political nous—it often involves trade-offs and by definition a buffer needs to focus on the needs and perspectives of one group, often at the

---

[4] Chris Ernst and Donna Chrobot-Mason, *Boundary Spanning Leadership*, New York, McGraw-Hill, 2011, pp. 92–103 and 172–196.

[5] Ibid., p. 92.

expense of a different group. It can be a lonely and isolating role, and as buffers often live out their role and responsibilities at the edge of an organization, or in the 'edgelands' themselves, it is a role best performed by strong, resilient individuals.

Weaving

The other tactic used in boundary spanning leadership that I'd like to flag here is that of 'weaving'. For Ernst and Chrobot-Mason, weaving occurs 'when group boundaries "interlace" yet remain distinct.'[6] As with a woven fabric in which individual threads are woven together to create a beautiful, integrated, greater whole, and yet each thread remains distinct, so this can be—metaphorically—the case in conscious collaboration. Repurposing the word 'weaving' is inspired, and evokes the image of something new being woven—or created—from the multiple threads, or we imagine two pieces of fabric being stitched together to create a single new piece. In both those examples the threads or pieces retain their individual distinctiveness, reflecting a unique aspect of conscious collaboration.

Weaving conveys the importance of uniqueness and diversity, which characterizes conscious collaboration. Collaboration isn't about a creating one homogeneous blend where individual distinctiveness and differences are merged into one—rather it's about celebrating diversity and really capitalizing on the differences, using them carefully and strategically to move the collaboration forward. So often we see collaborative endeavors smoothing over disagreement and not benefitting from the different perspectives, creativity, new ideas and approaches.

It is during the process of weaving and linking different sources of collaborative capacity that we begin to see possibilities for community emerge; interdependence increases and collaborative bonds become stronger. However, it is also during this process that the potential for conflict arises, and these require a great deal of courage, insight and strength from those who find themselves brokering a partnership or facilitating the collaboration. It is often at this time that the need for mediation

---

[6] Ibid., p. 178.

and constructive reconciliation becomes apparent, and the collaboration competencies that I outlined in Chap. 6 come to the fore.

The Bridge

Although the metaphor of weaving is entirely appropriate for conscious collaboration, there are still times when we arrive at the 'edgelands' seeking to collaborate, but it is not possible to discern a way over the chasm beneath us. At those moments we might start looking for a bridge.

When Abi and I were visiting our good friends in Laos back in 2011, we came across some quite amazing bamboo bridges that were used to span the tributaries of the Mekong and the Nam Khan river itself. They had been built in order to link communities and to access resources that lay out of reach. We learned many things from those simple bamboo bridges:

The metaphor of the bridge stuck with us and when Abi and I launched The Conscious Project in 2012 it became an icon for us and an important part of our story.

A Story About a Bridge

When you want to cross a river, you need to build a bridge. In many countries, people build bridges out of what they have to hand; the materials and tools they are familiar with.

Bamboo bridges are strong, flexible, perfectly suited to their surroundings and fit for their purpose.

While they stand, they are a tribute to the skill, resourcefulness and unique style of the people who built them. When they are washed away in the rainy season, they are recyclable and biodegradable. Next time, they are built better, with more understanding, skill and experience, maybe even more style.

What's on the other side?
What do you need to do to get to where you want to be?

Maybe it's time to build a better bridge?
From The Conscious Project website[7]

Agility

As I reflect on boundary spanning, it strikes me that agility is an important characteristic of those who are buffering, connecting, weaving or bridge-building. Agility in terms of thinking, and also in terms of behavior and practice. I mentioned that I had found living and working at the edge to be exhilarating and it's true that I find being next to (or in) the outdoors much more stimulating that being stuck inside! I find my ideas have more expression and can take form where the air is clearer. But it takes energy and agility—always looking, reflecting, evaluating, moving, seeking.

Being on the edge can also be a lonely place when collaboration does not materialize, or when ideas that you put out there do not land smoothly or find resonance with the people you meet. Being able to pick yourself up when you get knocked down requires strength of mind as well as a level of physical fitness. Collaboration is hard work, and the days can be long. We also need to recognize when we need to rest, retreat or regroup and be strong enough to do that.

Unusual Suspects

One characteristic of the various collaborations I have been involved in is the diversity of the people. I don't just mean in terms of ethnicity or gender or age—important though they are—I mean in terms of personalities, skill sets and competencies. Some of those people have been very different to me, and yet we were able to find a way of working together. From an external perspective, we were truly unusual suspects,[8] and I think that's

---

[7] Abi Green, The Conscious Project, essays, and in discussion with the author, December 2014 http://www.theconsciousproject.org/our-story/ (accessed December 15, 2014).

[8] The term 'unusual suspects' is one I first came across on these two websites: http://www.civicsystemslab.org and http://www.civicsystemslab.org/unusual-suspects-festival (accessed October 18, 2015).

an indicator for conscious collaboration. In many ways it's much easier to collaborate with someone who is just like us—especially if they are both a peer and a kindred spirit. Of course the collaboration might be conscious or unconscious, or both. But there is something about the intentionality and commitment required when we work with someone who is very different to us that sets those partnerships apart—collaboration between unusual suspects is a conscious decision and a conscious act, and it requires a relentless focus on the vision and outcomes, and a daily investment in the partnership itself.

Permission and Forgiveness

One feature of living on the porous edge and connecting across boundaries is the risk of causing offense, upsetting someone or getting into trouble. Although I generally take the view that offense can be more easily taken than given, it's also true that upsetting or irritating people, or getting oneself into trouble can be counter-productive in terms of catalyzing collaboration and it doesn't always help a collaborative venture to achieve its goal.

There's a saying attributed to Grace Murray Hopper, a computer programmer in the US Navy: 'It's easier to ask forgiveness than it is to get permission.'[9] It's an expression that has often been used by those working in technology and software development, but it has resonance for those of us who are involved in conscious collaboration. Sometimes, motivated perhaps by the collaborative vision, and a clear focus on the collaboration's desired outcome, individuals or partner organizations will say or do things that do more than create discomfort. Those moments call for humility and forgiveness. They are testing times for a partnership and this is one of the reasons why collaboration agreements and agreed operating principles can help: they can act as a guide in such situations, helping us navigate a principled and fair path through conflict and disagreement, and reminding us why we were collaborating in the first place.

The beginnings of collaboration tend to be organic and involve individuals stepping outside their comfort zones. Often it's a meeting of minds or

---

[9] https://en.wikiquote.org/wiki/Grace_Hopper (accessed October 18, 2015).

a connection around an emerging issue or a common challenge that needs to be addressed, and if we waited for permission to tackle such issues, we might find ourselves still on the start line; many of the breakthroughs achieved by collaborations over the decades would still be simply ideas.

One of the most successful collaborations I've been involved in is the NGO Local Pay.[10] It is an initiative which People In Aid (now the CHS Alliance) launched back in 2008 with the Birches Group and InsideNGO to support organizational effectiveness and operational excellence among international NGOs by creating readily available access to current, robust, relevant labor market data. It also builds capacity for good global management of reward. At the time there was a real shortage of high-quality pay data, with NGOs typically undertaking a local salary survey themselves or with a local consultancy firm, and with little consistency between country programs and even less between organizations. NGO Local Pay now counts more than 350 participating organizations in more than 80 countries, with a core group of more than 50 organizations committed to participating each year in all their countries. Since the launch back in 2008 more than 600 organizations have participated in at least one Local Pay survey. The NGO Local Pay partnership is a great example of conscious collaboration and making the most of a porous edge, in that each of the partners had to extend themselves beyond their normal boundaries. They made risk-based decisions and investments in an idea (a service) that theoretically would be a success and meet a clear need, but had never been achieved by anyone before. It is testament to the vision, commitment and tenacity of the partners, especially Curtis Grund and Warren Heaps at the Birches Group, that we managed to hold it together despite significant pressure from our bosses to deliver demonstrable financial returns as well as a providing a great service to our customers and users. Although the collaboration has evolved substantially since its creation, and now comprises two of the three original partners, it is nonetheless a success story, and delight. It is pleasing to see

---

[10] http://www.ngolocalpay.net (accessed October 18, 2015).

a growing number of subscribers benefit from affordable pay data as well as being able to participate in workshops to develop their reward expertise that are being held around the world.

But like most things that are worth doing, this collaboration was hard, and getting to the point of viability (and then beyond that to success), took a phenomenal amount of graft. In the early days I remember regularly meeting with Curtis and Warren in cafés and hotels in lower Manhattan and in East London, as well as the hours and hours of Skype calls, making product decisions, strategy decisions and committing to launch dates (and then each of us having to go back and explain to our bosses what we had committed to), negotiating ongoing support and a modest budget to enable us to meet again the next time and schedule a workshop or two. Looking back, I still flinch when I realize how close to the wind we sailed, and how close each partner was to 'pulling the plug' at various points along the way. We resorted to every tactic we knew in order to keep the partnership and collaboration alive—from collaboration agreements, shared operating principles, contracts, plenty of time invested as individuals, a good dose of humility, plenty of generosity, comfort with ambiguity and uncertainty and agility, too. At one critical junction, it became clear that I needed to fly to New York at only a few days' notice in order to resolve a tension that threatened to derail the collaboration. It was a big ask of my own boss at the time, not just in financial terms, but he could see how important it was and agreed to take the risk and fund the trip. In another café in on 42nd Street we thrashed out big issues and small print. And there was more than one occasion that colleagues at the Birches Group had to do the same. NGO Local Pay is a collaboration between unusual suspects too: at the beginning there was a fair amount of friction to overcome as a result of the very different personalities involved, and navigating the nonprofit vs. private sector dimension required sensitivity and understanding, for People In Aid (now the CHS Alliance) and the Birches Group are two organizations with very different origins, business models, types of revenue stream and governance/decision-making structures.

In Summary

Edges and boundaries are a fact of organizational life—but sometimes those edges are porous, allowing us to move from the inside to the outside. Sometimes the challenges we come across require us to build a bridge in order to reach a point of safety or stability where we might be able to initiate collaboration.

Opportunities for conscious collaboration often emerge beyond the porous edge of an organization, in other words conscious collaboration begins in the 'edgelands' that exist outside the organizational boundaries, where there may be fewer organizational norms and looser controls, and a heightened sense of the challenges or issues that need to be tackled collaboratively. Partnerships develop between unusual suspects who have the freedom to move outside of the traditional parameters, and who are motivated by a common cause. These individuals—the unusual suspects—are often better at seeking forgiveness than they are at asking for permission. And they are often agile—quick to spot opportunity and able to navigate risk.

Conscious collaboration has a lot in common with boundary spanning—and as with boundary spanning leaders, conscious collaborators need to be adept at buffering—protecting others from risk or threat and filtering communication in order that the team has space to think and act—and weaving—ensuring that the individual threads of collaboration are woven together to create a beautiful, integrated, greater whole, while retaining their individual distinctiveness.

For Reflection

As you think about the space beyond your organizational boundary—that is, the outside—why not take a few moments to reflect:

• When or where have you gone beyond the edge in order to collaborate?
• Who have you connected with in the 'edgelands'?
• What inspires you about what lies outside—or beyond—your organization and what scares you?

11

'Trust on Credit'

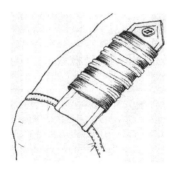

Introduction

Much of what's been written about collaboration focuses on the importance of trust: building it, developing it, maintaining it, breaking it, rebuilding it. And there's no doubt at all that it is absolutely central. An element of trust is required in even the most basic transaction or contract,

© The Editor(s) (if applicable) and The Author(s) 2016
B. Emmens, *Conscious Collaboration*,
DOI 10.1057/978-1-137-53805-5_11

but when partnerships form and conscious collaboration begins, with partners venturing out into the unknown, then it becomes essential.

We know from literature, research and personal experience that the level of trust in a team has a strong link with effective co-operation and collaboration, with morale, with flexibility, with knowledge transfer and learning, with participation, with innovation and creativity, with leadership effectiveness and with generally more productive and effective individual relationships. We also know that when trust breaks down, individuals often take fewer risks (preferring to protect themselves and play safe), administrative controls and checking procedures tend to increase, and important or sensitive information can be withheld, resulting in high levels of stress, communication gaps and a general deterioration in relationships, and of course, the organization or partnership suffers and the quality of work is affected.

In Chap. 5 I presented the notion of social and collaborative capital and how we could choose to venture or invest it in different situations. Some of those points apply equally for trust and I will explore that theme, along with the concept of the trust bank, in this chapter. I also want to introduce a couple of new ideas to help us reflect on our own approach to and understanding of trust. But first, what do we mean by trust?

Defining Trust

The *Oxford English Dictionary* defines trust as being a 'firm belief in the reliability, truth, or ability of someone or something',[1] and by that definition, trust encompasses both character and competence, and is indeed a prerequisite for collaboration.

It's helpful to elaborate a little further though, especially as it helps us understand why trust is so important. To help elaborate, I want to go back to my modest involvement in another ambitious collaborative initiative—the Emergency Capacity Building project[2]—which undertook some specific work on trust and produced an excellent toolkit for

---

[1] http://www.oxforddictionaries.com/definition/english/trust (accessed October 18, 2015).

[2] http://www.ecbproject.org (accessed October 18, 2015).

emergency response called 'Building Trust in Diverse Teams.'[3] which is available to download free.

My involvement in the Emergency Capacity Building project began back in 2007, again while I was working as a Director at People In Aid. My boss and I identified an opportunity for partnership with the project and the door was opened to us. In fact perhaps a better metaphor is the bridge metaphor, as it involved us at People In Aid and colleagues in the project team stepping outside of our normal work, extending ourselves and meeting mid-way, and defining a workplan that would enable the project to realize its objectives, and further our respective causes. As People In Aid's most senior HR specialist, I got involved in a number of projects relating to staff capacity and strategic human resources management and development and worked with a number of project teams—particularly during the first phase of the project.

The Emergency Capacity Building project was itself an unprecedented collaboration between aid agencies and in some respects it was the precursor to the Start Network in existence today. It aimed to improve the speed, quality and effectiveness of the humanitarian community to save lives, improve welfare and protect the rights of people in emergency situations. The project started in 2004 when emergency directors from seven agencies—CARE International, Catholic Relief Services, International Rescue Committee, Mercy Corps, Oxfam GB, Save the Children and World Vision International—met to discuss the most persistent challenges in humanitarian aid delivery. An Inter-Agency Working Group on Emergency Capacity was formed after this meeting and published a Report on Emergency Capacity the following year. It identified key capacity gaps constraining the ability to provide timely, effective and high-quality preparedness and response to emergencies. Following this, the initiative began, spanning 8 years (Phase I: 2005–2008 and Phase II: 2008–2013). Phase I of the project involved the development and publishing of more than 20 research findings, field tools and practical guides. Phase II continued to work toward meeting the overarching project goal of improving the speed, quality and effectiveness of the humanitarian community. It was one of

---

[3] http://policy-practice.oxfam.org.uk/publications/building-trust-in-diverse-teams-the-toolkit-for-emergency-response-115413 (accessed October 18, 2015).

the most ambitious collaborative projects the aid sector had seen—and it was made possible by the financial support of a number of donors including the Bill and Melinda Gates Foundation, the Microsoft Corporation, The European Commission's Humanitarian Aid and Civil Protection Directorate General (ECHO) and the British and American governments (UKAID and USAID) as well as several private donors.[4]

Building Trust in Diverse Teams

Early in Phase I of the Emergency Capacity Building project, the project team commissioned research by McKinsey and Company and found that trust between national and international staff was one of the single most important factors in an organization's ability to deliver a timely and effective emergency response. Subsequent work with two UK-based consulting groups—Castleton Consulting[5] and TCO International Diversity Management[6]—to research the definition of trust, resulted in a definition that outlined ten criteria for trust. The project is well worth a look, and the toolkit, although created nine years ago, is still very relevant and used regularly by aid agencies that undertake emergency response.

With reference to the 'Building Trust in Diverse Teams' toolkit,[7] the ten criteria for trust in summary are as follows:

- Competence—Trust based on a perception that team members are competent, and so will not let me down
- Openness with information—Trust based on the observation that other team members share information important to the team proactively and clearly
- Integrity—Trust based on the observation that other team members maintain promises, are team-orientated, and behave toward me in accordance with a moral code

---

[4] http://www.ecbproject.org/about.aspx (accessed October 18, 2015).

[5] http://castletonconsulting.co.uk (accessed October 18, 2015).

[6] http://www.tco-international.com (accessed October 18, 2015).

[7] http://policy-practice.oxfam.org.uk/publications/building-trust-in-diverse-teams-the-toolkit-for-emergency-response-115413 (accessed October 18, 2015).

- Reciprocity—Trust based on the observation that other team members are trusting and co-operative toward me
- Compatibility—Trust based on background, values, approaches, interests and objectives held in common
- Goodwill—Trust based on the belief that other team members are concerned about my overall welfare
- Predictability—Trust based on the observation that the behavior of team members is consistent over time and in different contexts
- Well-being—Trust arising from the feeling that I have nothing to fear from other members of the team
- Inclusion—Trust based on the observation that other team members actively include me in their social and work activities
- Accessibility—Trust based on the observation that other team members share their true feelings and I can relate to them on a personal level

Then, in what I think is one of the most helpful contributions to our understanding of trust, particularly in emergency response settings, the project team went on to sub-divide the ten criteria into two categories, according to whether they are swift trust or deeper trust. Swift trust can be readily achieved and is necessary from an early stage (competence, openness with information, integrity, reciprocity) whereas deeper trust takes more time to establish and requires focused effort on an ongoing basis (compatibility, goodwill, predictability, well-being, inclusion and accessibility).[8]

Trust on Credit

Stepping back up a level and thinking about trust in the broadest sense, we know that our own approach and attitude toward trusting others is our starting point, particularly when it comes to collaboration. We know that collaboration typically emerges as a result of two or more individuals choosing

---

[8] Oxfam GB, *Building Trust in Diverse Teams*, Oxford, Oxfam GB and the Emergency Capital Building Project, 2007, pp. 7–12.

to partner and tackle a shared issue or a new challenge. And although there are similarities with the way in which trust works with corporations, brands or other entities, it is in the interpersonal and in the collaborative relationship (as opposed to the customer/service relationship) that we can see the impact of our attitudes.

Recognizing this, I began to reflect on how I develop trust with others, and I discovered that what I was finding resonated with those I spoke to. My approach in general was to offer my trust up front, on credit as it were. I figured if I was generous and ventured some trust, that would likely be reciprocated. My decision to venture trust was like a down payment or deposit, that could be withdrawn (only without interest) if trust was broken. The key was that—provided certain basic criteria were met, and I wasn't dealing with a criminal or narcissist—the trust was offered unconditionally, and interest-free.

Some would say that I was crazy to do this, and that such an approach is both naïve and unsustainable. But we'll come to the alternatives in a moment, as while they exist, they are either equally naïve or much less appealing. I suppose I acted and continue to act from an abundance mindset or perspective. Trust is hard to quantify, but we have to continue to believe in people and trust them even when the evidence suggests we might want to do otherwise, or at least that we might want to hedge our trust until we can be certain we won't be disappointed. In my experience, despite the inevitable disappointments along the way, I have still benefitted hugely from offering trust on credit, with plenty of reciprocation and plenty of surprises, too. I've learnt to be sure to have a good exit strategy in the event things do go wrong, and I'm getting better at discerning where the trust will be taken and then my generosity will be exploited, but overall it's a much more satisfying and fulfilling way to live.

Another way of putting it is like this, in the words of Nurpur Singh, also a participant in the Future of Work Research Consortium: 'Trust someone until they are unworthy of trust.'[9] When we contemplate what that means, we realize that some fairly fundamental relationships exist on this basis—partnerships such as marriage or the relationship between a parent or carer and their children.

---

[9] Nurpur Singh, cited by Lynda Gratton in *The Key*, London, McGraw-Hill, 2014, p. 70.

I coined the term 'trust on credit' a while back; friends would hear me talk about it and ask me what I meant by it. But it wasn't until February 2012 when I was at a Future of Work masterclass on complex collaboration, being run by Lynda Gratton's Hot Spots Movement,[10] that it really came to life. I'd been using the term to describe the way in which I approached new business partnerships, particularly drawing on my experience working at People In Aid which required me to continually seek new partnership possibilities and collaborative opportunities.

'Earning Your Trust Stripes'

One of the catalysts that prompted me to think about trust differently was an experience back in my mid-twenties when I was working in Switzerland with the Union Cycliste Internationale—the world governing body for the sport of cycling. At the time I had a senior colleague who had spent his early career in the military, and occasionally, when we were working together and I'd not quite met his expectations, he would—true to the stereotype of a military general—lose his temper with me and give me a tongue-lashing. I did my best to avoid that eventuality, and looking back I can see that I was working hard to 'earn my trust stripes'. Each time I did something that pleased him I would notch up another 'trust stripe', and each success or achievement gradually built trust. There wasn't a whole lot of 'trust on credit' given to me in that job—I had to earn the trust on a daily basis, and there was always the risk of demotion.

And in a way, the metaphor of having to 'earn your trust stripes' is one that also applies to many different organizations, brands and contexts, especially where trust has been broken. It's certainly true for the Union Cycliste Internationale and the sport of cycling today. The 1990s were a dark time for cycling and significant trust issues—particularly relating to blood doping—emerged for the sport itself as well as for the governing body and national federations. Sadly those trust issues were to get a lot worse during the early 2000s and it's really only in the last few years that

---

[10] http://www.hotspotsmovement.com/research-institute.html (accessed October 18, 2015).

we've seen concerted efforts by all parties to earn back trust in the sport and in those who govern it.

I don't think trust really exists as a latent, finite entity—it's fluid, dynamic and something that can be grown or diminished, even to the point of disappearing. Conscious collaboration is often a blend of trust offered (whether on credit or in exchange) and trust earned. It helps to be mindful of this, and to be conscious of how what we do (or don't do) affects trust in the collaboration.

'Vicarious Trust'

There's another type of trust that those collaborating might often come across—it's what I call 'vicarious trust'. Vicarious trust arises when someone we trust in turn recommends or endorses someone else, and we take that on good authority and accordingly extend a level of trust to that third party.

I'd argue that vicarious trust can be a good thing—and in the context of collaboration especially it can be a powerful force for good, but as with many things there is also another side.

Clearly there are some potential risks associated with vicarious trust: isn't that how old boys' networks and other exclusive societies work? In a way it is—once you're in then you're definitely in, and you become bound by their code and traditions, and loyal even to the oath of omertà. Opportunities for outsiders to join are virtually nonexistent and unfair—sometimes illegal—Discrimination is rife. So we need to be very careful.

But I want to go back for a moment and highlight the potential benefits of vicarious trust. In a conscious collaboration the ability to transparently and fairly onboard new partners to the collaboration, based on existing members' social capital, is tremendously positive and can give the collaboration a substantial advantage over competitors, as well as increasing the chances of success. It can do this by increasing the pool of partners, bringing in new competencies and capacities and contributing to the creative process. Vicarious trust is also a potential indicator of a new partner being a good behavioral fit, and in the early stages of a collaboration it can speed up the process of mobilization and ensure the collaboration gets underway quickly and efficiently.

And in a way, vicarious trust exists for organizations too: when we look at ratings and reviews of other organizations before entering into a partnership we are looking at what others think and making ourselves open to being influenced by their view or opinion. Granted, we commission due diligence and also look at wider reputational issues as we gather our evidence, but when an organization or institution we respect and trust vouches for a potential partner, then we take that on good authority. And it's right to do this. One word of warning though—vicarious trust is an important element of conscious collaboration but we must seek to remain open to collaboration with new partners, and avoid reverting to closed networks that risk unfair discrimination and limit the potential of collaboration. Misusing vicarious trust—that is using it to justify a retreat back to a known and familiar place—seals the porous edge and means we are likely to miss exciting opportunities that lie beyond it.

The Trust Bank

In Chap. 5, when we were looking at social capital, I made a reference to the metaphor of the bank account, put forward by Stephen Covey in his book *The 7 Habits of Highly Effective People*.[11] Covey writes about the emotional bank account and makes reference to 'the reserve of trust which is maintained by regular deposits.'[12] I'd like to return to that metaphor here and make no apology for drawing on Covey's work again; his contribution to our understanding of trust is profoundly important and if you're looking to explore trust in greater depth then he covers the subject comprehensively.

In conscious collaboration, we need to pay attention to the trust bank balance, and ensure that we are, in Covey's words, making regular deposits. Trust is largely built through small acts of generosity, a word of appreciation, choosing to hold back momentarily and focus on actively listening, or when we put someone else's interests above ours, or walked alongside a colleague during a particularly difficult or bumpy part of

---

[11] Stephen R. Covey, *The 7 Habits of Highly Effective People*, London, Simon & Schuster, 1989.
[12] Ibid., p. 188.

the journey—those are the deposits I'm talking about. David Hieatt of the Do Lectures says in his 'manifesto of a doer': 'Little actions repeated relentlessly result in big change. Don't underestimate the importance of "small" multiplied by "often".'[13] Small multiplied by often is indeed important, especially where building trust is concerned.

'Miles in the Legs'

Over winter, many keen cyclists concentrate on 'getting the miles in their legs' in order to be ready for the start of a new racing season. I love this saying and use it far too often, particular when talking about work or life experience. As we've seen, trust is built through small things done often, and collaborative experience comes from—well—doing collaboration actually! One of the challenges we face, both in terms of building trust as well as gaining experience in collaboration, is that we do need to 'do the hours' or actually have the experience.

I regularly mentor young managers in their early to mid-twenties—it's inspiring and the benefits are mutual in that I surely gain as much from the encounters as they say they do. One thing that strikes me, though, is how keen most of them are to progress quickly in their career, and get promoted to a more senior role. The recurring question is along the lines of 'based on your experience, how can I speed up this process?', in other words, 'are there any short cuts?' At that point I smile inwardly and think about what it took me, how I can share that in a constructive way, and how I can reframe the question. In truth though, 15 years' experience takes fifteen years, and while we might be able to condense some experience or undergo a period of accelerated learning, whichever way we look at it we still can't get away from that truth. It's like the 'miles in the legs' analogy. In conscious collaboration the experience is hard earned and acquired over time. If we have put in the work, then we will be in a good position to be able to contribute to the collaboration.

---

[13] http://davidhieatt.typepad.com/doonethingwell/2014/12/a-manifesto-of-a-doer.html (accessed October 18, 2015).

'Trust Breeds Magic'

Tina Roth Eisenberg, founder of Creative Mornings[14] and Do Lectures alumni, takes the view that 'trust breeds magic',[15] and this is a delightful way of describing the culture we build when we are generous with our trust and actively seek to strengthen it.

As we've seen, we build trust primarily through our behaviors, but at a certain point the influence of trust can extend more widely, and encompass policies and procedures. When policies and procedures are based on high levels of trust, we give people freedom and space to perform. Such autonomy is highly regarded by many staff, and seen as a positive factor in increasing employee engagement. We certainly know that with the opposite of autonomy—that is to say tight controls and checks, micromanagement and little freedom to exercise initiative or be creative— morale suffers and engagement falls. We also know that when the climate of trust deteriorates and begins to break down, we often seek to compensate through more controls, regulations and supervision. The space for creativity shrinks, there is less room for movement and agility is reduced. So there are important lessons here for conscious collaboration, and those of us who initiate or broker partnerships and collaborative activity must pay attention not only to the culture of trust in behavioral terms, but also to the way in which systems, policies and procedures strengthen trust or conversely undermine it.

Dealing with Disappointment

If we are committed to collaborating, then sooner or later, we will find that our trust will be broken or that we were misguided in trusting someone or something. At that point we will have to deal with the disappointment of being let down, deceived or taken advantage of. In such

---

[14] You can find out more about the brilliantly collaborative Creative Mornings movement here http://www.creativemornings.com (accessed October 18, 2015).

[15] http://www.thedolectures.com/tina-roth-eisenberg-trust-breeds-magic/#.ViTyrdZcIsw (accessed October 18, 2015).

circumstances, it's entirely possible that the breakdown of trust may be final and irrevocable, though I believe that is often a matter of perspective and attitude, especially in cases where we have been careful with due diligence and partner selection. However, the way we deal with the disappointment and breakdown of trust may be the deciding factor in whether trust can be rebuilt or not.

There's a reason why humility is a core value of conscious collaboration—and it applies to all parties. When trust breaks down there is inevitably more than one side to the story. As a wise friend once said to me—'there's at least two sides, and then somewhere in there is the truth.' Rebuilding trust therefore requires intentionality and humility: a commitment to rebuild is a prerequisite, and humility is required to acknowledge the circumstances around the breakdown.

Collaboration agreements along with agreed operating principles can be of great help here—I can recall a few partnerships where an inadvertent act—or the unintended consequences of an action carried out in good faith—caused upset and the trust we'd taken time to establish took a battering. Each time it was the fact we were able to look to our founding principles, and the reason why we had come together in the first place, and what we were aiming to achieve, that enabled us to apologize, deal with the consequences of the action and rebuild the relationship to move forwards.

We owe it to our conscious collaborations to ensure they are sturdy and resilient enough to be able to weather the inevitable storms that will come—that means actively building trust and making deposits in the trust bank at every opportunity. It also means—realistically—that we need to be prepared for the possibility of being disappointed (in advance) so that we have a strategy and action plan for dealing with the consequences and the rebuilding afterwards.

In Summary

In this chapter we've looked at the importance of trust in conscious collaboration, how we define it and the criteria for trust. We know that when trust is lacking or absent, space and autonomy decrease and controls and surveillance increase, which in turn can affect the quality of work and cause interpersonal relationships to suffer. Fundamentally, low-trust environments are not enjoyable places to be and for many are associated with all sorts of toxic behaviors. High-trust environments on the other hand are typically places of high performance, commitment and engagement; places where magic can happen.

As conscious collaborators we have a responsibility to play our own part in building trust by making regular deposits in the trust bank. One of the ways in which we can do this is through small acts of generosity repeated often. It's also important that we honor commitments and demonstrate active listening.

When trust is broken, we also have a responsibility to act with maturity and in humility, acknowledging when we are at fault and choosing to play our part in rebuilding trust in order to achieve the vision and outcomes the collaboration is striving for.

For Reflection

As you think about trust, building trust, offering trust and rebuilding trust, why not take a few moments to reflect:

- On which occasions have you been the first to trust?
- Who is waiting for you to trust them?
- Do you offer trust on credit or does your trust have to be hard earned?
- What can you do to strengthen trust in your existing collaborations?

12

'Jamming'

Introduction

Chapter 11 emphasized importance of trust in conscious collaboration and there's no doubt at all in my mind that it is one of the most important elements. This chapter takes a step beyond trust to explore what becomes possible when trust is the foundation.

© The Editor(s) (if applicable) and The Author(s) 2016
B. Emmens, *Conscious Collaboration*,
DOI 10.1057/978-1-137-53805-5_12

For me, 'jamming' is one of those things that becomes possible when there is a foundation of trust, and it is an exciting aspect of conscious collaboration. Next, we will take a look at what 'jamming' means, how we 'jam' and what results we might expect if we are bold enough to give it a go!

What Is Jamming?

When I mention jamming—or the possibility of running a jam—to a colleague I'm often met with a slightly bewildered look which soon turns to intrigue, and then to questions: What does that even mean? Is it allowed? How…? When…? Can we…? It's usually those with a vaguely musical background that have been the first to realize my meaning: jamming is a term that tends to be associated with jazz music, and is taken to mean improvising music with other musicians. Today, and in the context of collaboration in the workplace, jamming is usually taken to mean an online collaborative discussion about business or social issues. You may have come across similar processes—a colleague recently referred to an 'ideas crunch', and many of my colleagues regularly participate in 'hackathons', in bring people together to engage in collaborative computer programming and software design.

To the best of my knowledge, it is a term that IBM introduced back in 2003, when it used an online platform to enable its workforce to participate in the redefining of its core values for the first time in 100 years—the online event was called ValuesJam.[1] I personally first came across the term back in 2006 when I was invited to join another IBM online jam—this time it was the InnovationJam, and it entailed pulling together more than 150,000 people from 104 countries and 67 companies. It was a huge undertaking.

At the time I was astonished by the scale of such a collaborative endeavor—it was still the early days of Web 2.0—Facebook had been launched in 2004 and Twitter in 2006—and that level of social interaction was relatively unknown, or at least confined to niche communities

[1] https://www.collaborationjam.com (accessed October 1, 2015).

in Silicon Valley and other tech-hubs. But I admired the audacious ambition and was curious about how jams could be applied in the aid sector.

Jams captured my imagination as they seemed to be the embodiment of conscious collaboration, and although they were online—thus limiting participation to those who had access—they seemed to be a perfect catalyst for harnessing the creativity of a specific group on a specific issue or topic. The notion of a focused conversation over a fixed period of time, with the aim of achieving very practical outcomes was captivating, and in many ways it was the precursor to some of the crowd-sourcing initiatives we see today. When combined with powerful software to enable data analysis, jams enabled management teams to identify the core issues and gain insight to where the group's energy lay and which issues were actually the most important to allocate for discussion time and comments.

Online jams are an excellent collaboration tool for communication, awareness and cultural change, but to achieve their potential they must also be seen as part of a process. They require careful planning beforehand, real clarity about their core intent and purpose and deliberate follow-up. In fact the follow-up is critical, and today jams are often an important stage in the formation of community.

Jamming and Conscious Collaboration

I see jamming as a critical component of conscious collaboration. In my own work over the last ten years or so I have stretched the concept to include face-to-face or audio jams in which we harness the creativity of a specific group on a specific issue or topic, and for a specific time. Jams of this nature require courageous, humble and confident facilitation—they don't always work, although they can exceed anyone's expectations.

Key to success is the support and commitment of a client who 'gets it' and sees the potential that a jam can offer, which is a huge return for a condensed and finite investment. With good facilitation and meticulous planning, jams enable diverse stakeholders to tackle major challenges or conundrums and to co-create collaborative ways forward that will ultimately deliver positive outcomes.

One of the most successful jams I ran was back in the summer of 2011 when a small group of people came together in a room in London for a day to collaboratively design a multi-day learning event for a major nonprofit client—a consortium of humanitarian INGOs. The learning event we were designing would run consecutively in five different countries, engaging participants and a wider stakeholder group in each location and gradually building up a body of knowledge and insight that would enable the uptake of learning by a much wider community. It was one of the most productive, exhilarating and focused days of work I have ever experienced, and was followed up by the production of a learning event handbook and facilitation guide which were instrumental in enabling the events to run successfully later that year.

Learning to Jam

The jam I mentioned above was in some ways more successful than the jam I'd convened the previous year for a different consortium of INGOs. I've already highlighted the importance of a commitment to 'always be learning', and that was as true for me in 2010 as it is today! In 2010 I found myself in the role of lead consultant for the design of two innovative humanitarian development programs (briefly mentioned in Chap. 6): a core skills program and a management and leadership program. Having successfully worked to deliver a widely accepted and acclaimed core competencies framework, attention shifted to the design and implementation of these two programs which would be piloted in four countries over the course of 18 months, and People In Aid had successfully bid to lead the design, development and implementation. The work—which became known as the Context Project[2]—was being led by Oxfam on behalf of what was then called the Consortium of British Humanitarian Agencies and which has since evolved into the Start Network.[3] Again I worked with the indefatigable Sara Swords and together with an inspiring project

---

[2] http://contextproject.org (accessed October 1, 2015).
[3] www.startnetwork.org (accessed October 1, 2015).

manager at Oxfam—Caroline Hotham—we created what I think each of us would agree was a 'conscious collaboration'.

At an early stage I remember persuading Caroline to agree to host a jam in Oxford to which we would invite some of the best learning program designers we knew, plus a handful of other interesting individuals, and set about scoping the programs and identifying important program characteristics and elements. In some ways it was quite a scrappy process, in that it was untidy, stuttering and at times vague—not everyone was clear why they were there although clarity did emerge during our time together. However, in the weeks and months that followed we realized that we had achieved something quite remarkable out of the jam. Not only did we have a clear idea of the scope and shape of the programs and a fair bit of content, we also saw that we had engaged supporters of the work and secured some valuable buy-in and commitment to see the programs through to successful delivery and implementation. A number of the original jammers stuck with us and we jammed again a few more times. Of the initial group, some ended up facilitating pilot programs in countries such as disparate as Bolivia, Bangladesh, Indonesia and Kenya.

In retrospect, jamming provided the foundation for one of the most ambitious collaborative projects I have been involved with in the aid sector. I owe it to Caroline Hotham for having faith and seeing the potential of the process. Her trust in me, Sara and the team, and her outstanding project management skills were central to the success of the collaboration.

I've also learnt a huge amount about jamming from Lynda Gratton who leads the Future of Work Research Consortium under the auspices of the Hot Spots Movement.[4] I've enjoyed being a part of that learning community and one of the aspects I've appreciated most have been the online jams—FoWLab Jams.[5] For the Future of Work Research Consortium, jams are 'a guided online conversation that harnesses the collaborative intelligence of [...] employees, applies cutting-edge analytics software to this conversation and then present[s] you with a report

---

[4] http://www.hotspotsmovement.com (accessed October 1, 2015).
[5] http://www.hotspotsmovement.com/future-of-work.html (accessed October 1, 2015).

containing actionable results.'[6] However, what is clear from the IBM and FoWLab jams, as well as from my own learning, is that a jam is only one of a suite of tools, techniques and processes used to enable collaborative conversations and harness the creativity of a large group.

I've also learnt a lot through experimenting with one-to-one jamming, that is, jamming as a pair, typically in the form of 'walk and talk' events. There's something about movement and ideas, inspiration and creativity, especially when outdoors and surrounded by nature. In the past I'd often spent time coaching or being coached while walking—I like the visual cues and the way in which physical landmarks offer metaphorical milestones or stages in thinking and progress, and the same principles applied when jamming away on specific ideas or issues. Walks tend to be finite, in that they have a beginning and end, and so they lend themselves to a time-bound burst of creative energy, and the co-active nature of the conversation can be extremely productive.

More recently Abi and I have jointly facilitated small-scale jams with nonprofit clients in various situations and contexts and as we become more practiced and more confident, so we become more able to articulate the purpose and benefits of jamming to those with whom we collaborate. We've enjoyed some success in developing curricula for frontline health and humanitarian staff using these methods, and in contributing to the establishment of a virtual academy for humanitarian workers.

Our current approach to jamming tends to blend synchronous and asynchronous online interaction with a face-to-face event, and to allow for some physical movement (for example a walk and talk) at some point during the jam for those who are gathered face to face. Props and tools can be useful, and apart from the ubiquitous Post-it* notes and Sharpie* pens, and plentiful supplies of good coffee and chocolate brownies, The Conscious Project is a big fan of John Willshire's invention the 'Artefact cards'[7]—small, high-quality, colorful packs of blank playing cards—which we have used with clients, associates and partners all over the world to capture ideas and thinking, and to collaboratively design and plan.

---

[6] Ibid.

[7] http://artefactshop.com/pages/about (accessed October 1, 2015).

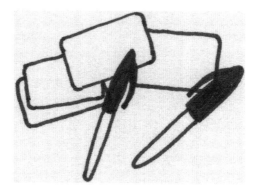

Fig. 12.1   Props and tools

How Do We Make Jams Work?

The ingredients for a successful jam are fairly straightforward: in addition to the courageous, humble and confident facilitation the main ingredients are planning, planning and then planning. Jamming requires a reasonably long lead time to ensure the people you need can schedule time to participate, and it needs a clear focus, that is to say the issue or theme/s you are addressing must be clearly set out, along with any problem statement or provocation.

Jamming works well when participants have already had previous opportunity to interact, whether in a meeting, workshop or event or in a conference call. In an online community, basic user or participant profiles can help to build trust as participants can see who else is joining the conversation. For online jams powerful analytics are essential and that often means partnering with a firm that has the technology to support the analysis and write-up.

For facilitators, the ability to actively listen and take good notes, as well as strong intuition, a high degree of comfort with uncertainty and ability to trust the process (collaborative conversations can go in all sorts of direction), and the courage to act in the moment are all important attributes.

Finally, I want to reiterate that freedom, creativity and improvization often come from a sound underpinning structure, a community that that trusts each other, and a clear focus on the issues and the desired out-come. Jam convenors and facilitators need to be good at scene-setting and drawing participants into the 'why we are here' and encouraging them to unlock their best topic-focused thinking, and *share* it.

The Downside to Jamming

One of the biggest downsides to jamming—particularly online jam-ming—is that it is not as inclusive as it could be, due to constraints or limitations relating to access and participation.

Conscious collaboration often involves working on a difficult social or environmental issue, which in turn means that some stakeholders, par-ticularly those in remote or less well-off communities, may have limited resources and be unable to participate. Online jams require reliable inter-net connectivity and access to a device which can browse the internet. Technological literacy may also be limited to certain demographic groups, for example those in education or with jobs and livelihoods which require them to be computer literate. In some communities elderly people, chil-dren and young people and groups that are marginalized may be unable to give their valuable input to the collaborative process. Face-to-face jams typically require mobility and the ability to access transport infrastruc-ture, and in some cases a way of traveling across borders (for example a passport and visa).

If you're thinking of using a jam as part of your conscious collabora-tion, care is needed to ensure it's an appropriate tool, that opportunities for participation are maximized and barriers removed wherever possi-ble. There may be other ways of ensuring collaboration and participa-tion, for example through using action research[8]—a term first coined by Kurt Lewin in the 1940s which basically means research that leads to social action. Action research is often extremely collaborative and can be accompanied by collective reflection and action planning—it lends itself to difficult issues that need a consciously collaborative approach such

---

[8] https://en.wikipedia.org/wiki/Action_research (accessed October 1, 2015).

as 'Women's Leadership in INGOs',[9] an action research project recently undertaken by Katy Murray and Sarah Fraser.

In my experience, jamming also has a habit of unleashing disagreement or dissent which, depending on your viewpoint, could be considered a downside or a positive. Handled poorly, it is a downside, in that trust could be irreparably impacted, participants could take offense and leave, or the process could simply stall and fail. It's vital that at such moments facilitators or brokers avoid 'smoothing'—that is smoothing over the disagreement and seeking superficial consensus—and it's important to recognize that these situations often require mediation and constructive reconciliation. Handled well—that is to say when facilitators act responsibly, carefully and respectfully, allowing diverse views to surface and be considered objectively and constructively—then it is a positive! In fact, going off-piste as a result of such an intervention can be very good indeed, and in many ways it is in the spirit of improvization! Most detours benefit from being contextualized by facilitators, and if the participants are able to harness the energy and animation of the group for positive impact, and provided the facilitator doesn't panic, then the new inputs can contribute to a better outcome!

Creative Events

The principles that underpin jamming can of course be woven into any event and, done well, this creates opportunities for conscious collaboration. One such event is the Do Lectures.[10] This has a cult following and is now run in the USA, the UK and Australia, with ambition for events further afield, too. Abi and I joined the Do Lectures back in 2013 and certainly for me it was an eye-opener. It was a small group, and while it seemed unlikely that a massive collaboration would emerge, we met with other entrepreneurs, and found inspiration. Some of the early seeds of conscious collaboration were sown at that event on a Welsh farm and

---

[9] http://www.resonateconsulting.co.uk/Site_2/Women_in_Leadership.html (accessed October 1, 2015).

[10] http://thedolectures.com (accessed October 1, 2015).

from that, and the wider Do Lectures community, exciting possibilities are emerging for many people.

The Do Lectures: In Their Words

It all started with an idea. A simple idea. Just a tiny seed. In their clever country called Wales, Clare and David Hieatt set out to bring the DO-ers of the world together—the movers and shakers, the disrupters and the change-makers—and ask them to tell their stories. Under starlit skies, in a bind with nature, they would inspire others to go out into the world and DO, too. The intent was that pure, the motivation honest.

In 2008, The DO Lectures was born, in an inexplicable cross-section between a festival and a conference. There were no name badges, no bad coffee and impersonal, drafty lecture halls. Instead, an intimate number of speakers and attendees gathered under canvas on the west coast of Wales and shared the whole three-day experience as a community. They ate together, camped together, shared a beer together around a fire as the sun went down. That intangible but very real spirit is kinda what makes us different from everything else.

Every year since, DO has stuck to the same formula: ideas + energy = change. Inspiring speakers, an engaged class of attendees and a beautiful location. It's a potent cocktail, and one that works. Year in, year out, people arrive with their tents and their dreams and leave 3 days later with a shift so profound it's been said that DO changed their lives.

In Summary

In a high-trust environment, jamming is an exciting aspect of conscious collaboration and one that enables a diverse community to engage in collaborative discussion around a specific topic or topics, and to harness the creativity and innovative ideas of the group members. Jamming is all about focused collaborative conversations with very practical outcomes, and it harnesses the power and wisdom of the crowd effectively. Jamming began as an online tool and process, and while online jams remain popular, the principles of jamming can be incorporated with creative face-to-face events to good effect.

It's important to remember that jamming is a process that requires planning and preparation, thoughtful inputs and provocations, sound analysis and a clear follow-up. Care should be taken to ensure barriers to participation are removed or lowered wherever possible, and where critical stakeholder voices are unlikely to be heard during a jam, then alternative methods for enabling those inputs should be found.

Finally, jams are learning processes; they require courageous, insightful, humble yet confident facilitation, and don't come with a guarantee of success. However, they are effective at building engagement, commitment and community, and exposing and extracting real and useful inputs from the participants, so if a jam doesn't quite go to plan, there's always next time!

For Reflection

As you think about jamming and the possibilities it offers for conscious collaboration, why not take a few moments to reflect:

* How could you introduce the concept of jamming to your collaborations?
* Where might your partners be open to jamming?
* Which issues that you are wrestling with lend themselves to a jam?

13

'The Virtual Guild'

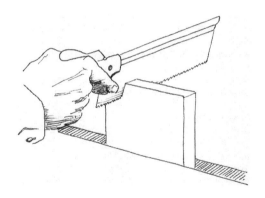

© The Editor(s) (if applicable) and The Author(s) 2016
B. Emmens, *Conscious Collaboration*,
DOI 10.1057/978-1-137-53805-5_13

Introduction

This chapter—the final of Part II—begins by reflecting on the early stages of The Conscious Project's creation of a virtual guild of master crafts-women and craftsmen, which could be a new model for conscious collaboration. I'll look at some other similar examples and consider the options available for small enterprises that seek to collaborate consciously in the face of competition from much larger firms.

What Is a Virtual Guild?

Virtual as a word has become quite firmly established in the English language, and is often taken to refer to that which is online, as in virtual academies or universities, virtual worlds, virtual reality games, and more. Early on it conjured up a sense of something which existed in a parallel world, but which somehow wasn't real in the sense of a tangible, face-to-face interaction. Much of that preconception may have been based on misunderstanding or ignorance—for as our engagement and familiarity with the digital realm has evolved, we now see that virtual is, for the most part, entirely 'real' and in the Western world at least, we have come to rely on it for routine daily tasks such as buying groceries, making video calls and shopping.

The notion of a virtual guild, however, is relatively recent, and to date I have come across very few definitions. It's a concept that I find very exciting, and it's a concept that we have tried to bring to life at The Conscious Project, although I do not claim ownership of the term. It was in a conversation with Ian Gee[1] back in early 2010 that I first came across it, as part of my preparation for a conference for humanitarian HR managers on the theme of 'talent management'. I was introduced to Ian by a mutual acquaintance a little before that—in 2009—and we quickly realized we had common interests and much to talk about, especially in the context of networks and communities. Ian had also participated in

---

[1] Ian Gee, Edgelands Consultancy in conversation with the author in Spring 2010. See http://www.edgelandsconsultancy.com (accessed October 1, 2015).

the Hot Spots Movement's Future of Work Research Consortium (led by Lynda Gratton) that I have previously mentioned. Ian had spent the previous couple of years as Director of Organization Development at Nokia and he and a colleague had agreed to come and share some of the learning about workplace communities.

It was in those early planning conversations with Ian that I got excited about what a virtual guild could mean for small, agile companies and networks that were seeking to compete with much larger and better-resourced entities. For me, the virtual guild is based on the principle of establishing open networks in which, built on shared understanding, those with appropriate competencies and capacities (skills, trades, knowledge, expertise, credentials) choose to come together to be stronger, sustainable, more effective and to achieve a desired outcome.

Guilds: The Early Beginnings

One thing that interests me deeply is how guilds emerged in rural and urban communities in the past. Some of the earliest records of guilds in Europe go back to medieval times when there were typically two types of guild—one for merchants (traders, sellers, dealers) and one for craftspeople (skilled workers with an occupation, artisans and 'makers'). Guilds flourished in the Middle Ages—primarily between the eleventh and sixteenth centuries—and played a very important role in both the economic and social fabric at that time.[2] Prior to that, and in Roman times, a form of craft guilds existed—known as collegia[3]—but they appear to have been primarily a way of controlling trades and raising tax revenue.

In Europe during the Middle Ages, guilds typically united a single type of industry or commerce, such as masons or architects in the building trade, or smiths, bakers, butchers or clothmakers. Although guilds emerged in order to ensure a monopoly of trade, they also ensured quality standards were met and prices remained stable. They were, however,

---

[2] http://www.britannica.com/topic/guild-trade-association (accessed October 1, 2015).
[3] Ibid.

primarily intended to serve the interests of the members and achieve economic objectives.

Guilds still exist today along similar lines, and those founding principles remain true—they enable members to stand up to stiff competition from outsiders, protect the economic interests of members and provide some guarantee of quality and craftsmanship.

Variations on the Guild

These days there are a few variations on the guild: when I first began work senior managers and those in business development, marketing or communications were easily identifiable by the Rolodex[4] on their desk—a contact management system that enabled the alphabetic storage and easy retrieval of business cards. In HR most recruiters had what they referred to colloquially as their 'black book'—a book containing a list of useful and important contacts.

In my early days of working with the humanitarian team at Save the Children on emergency responses, most people in the team—and certainly all recruiters—had a black book and those books were well thumbed indeed. They ensured we could find people at short notice to deploy on life-saving programs. Black books were guarded jealously and details of contacts shared cautiously.

In the private sector, while working at the Design Research Unit, again, everyone in a management or leadership role had their own black book which contained prized contact details for consultants, journalists, procurement managers and more, as well as all sorts of other secrets! Again, black books were precious and carefully looked after—after all, they were a compendium of social capital and the bigger the book, the more valuable you were to your team, your organization and the cause.

With the relative demise of the guild, and the rise of technological platforms and social media that have provided alternative ways of networking knowledge and expertise, professional and trades associations and other interest networks have evolved and assumed most of the role that guilds

---

[4] http://rolodex.com/products/contact-management (accessed October 1, 2015).

played, continuing to defend the interests of members, drive profession-alization and recognition, as well as upholding quality standards.

Redefining the Guild

When I reflected on what guilds stood for, and why they existed, I saw that in some ways they still have a great deal to offer, and yet in other ways they go against what we are trying to achieve. They are about intentional collaboration, but they were primarily for individual or group interests, and they didn't always seem to be about collaboration for the collective good, or conscious collaboration. I started to think about which bits of the model we could hack, and together with Abi, my co-director at The Conscious Project, we began to play around with a few ideas. What if we were able to find a way of linking and con-necting different trades—master craftspeople with different skills and expertise working in different industries—but all with a common goal of helping individuals and organizations think about what they were doing, and thereby making the world a better place? By definition that would have to be a virtual guild as the members would be scattered all over the globe, linked by technology and occasional joint assignments. How could we make that work? And moreover, how could we make our virtual guild work while avoiding the darker side of guilds which were notorious for their lack of transparency, and for their nepotism, self-interest and general impenetrability?

The Conscious Project's Virtual Guild

When Abi and I launched The Conscious Project in 2012 we were aware that interest in 'conscious' was about to break into the mainstream. Disappointment with political leaders, the banking crisis, growing aware-ness of the reality and impact of climate change and rising inequality were all contributing to animated debate and it was clear to many that the human race needed to rethink its approaches and actions in the face of such challenges.

It remains clear to us both that the only realistic hope we have as a race is to figure out conscious collaboration. The alternatives just aren't viable: no single person or company, not even the richest or biggest, has the resources or knowledge to tackle those issues alone. We need a systems approach that recognizes complexity, rather than discrete technocratic interventions; the world's systems and local communities generally are more interdependent than ever before and on top of all that it's simply very lonely indeed being a single voice campaigning or working on any of these challenging issues. We need each other to thrive, to share ideas, to hold us accountable, no matter whether we are introvert or extrovert, and no matter where in the world we are based. Of course, individuals here and there might choose to go off-grid for a time, but they are usually exceptional cases.

However, having respectively come from a small nonprofit and a large public sector organization we had no immediate desire to create a new large organization ourselves, along with all the financial responsibilities and compliance requirements that would entail. We needed to think differently. And so we began to think about how we could reappropriate and redefine the notion of the guild—creating a twenty-first-century version in the form of a virtual guild that connected experts from different fields who were at the top of their game, renowned for their insight and committed to excellence. If we could do that, we reasoned, we would still be able to work collaboratively on exciting projects that would achieve positive social outcomes. We figured that there were plenty of people around who would meet our criteria, it was just a matter of finding them, and connecting with them, and pitching what we were aiming to achieve to them and how they could be a part of it. One thing we did know was that such individuals were often already working very consciously, trying to ensure a balance in their lives in terms of their work portfolio and other commitments, not motivated solely by financial gain and committed to collaboration. We also knew that typically such people were expensive to hire due to their reputation and expertise and not necessarily available or open to being employed by us (we couldn't afford them, they valued their freedom and autonomy as an independent too much, or they were already happily employed). And so the (virtual) foundations of our virtual guild were laid, and we made a commitment to seek to work consciously and collaboratively wherever and whenever we could, in the hope that we would be able to demonstrate a new way of working.

So far, so good. Small beginnings, but they've been very encouraging and it's largely a result of our virtual guild that The Conscious Project is viable and beginning to achieve some exciting outcomes and bring about positive social change. It helps that we don't require large offices or real estate to do our work, nor do we need to house a large number of workers; all we really need to get started is a laptop computer and phone, electricity, an internet connection and our pens and notebooks. And an optimistic, enquiring attitude!

David and Goliath

Looking around today we see plenty of stories that are similar to ours— individuals and entrepreneurs making a go of things and starting up new businesses and ventures. They may be prompted by different events or changing personal situations, redundancy, a lack of job or career opportunities, new family circumstances or a desire to change the world that can be repressed no longer. Whatever the origins, those of us who find ourselves in that position can't help but feel that we are in a kind of David and Goliath situation,[5] that is to say, we have to face up to much bigger, stronger, better-resourced competitors.

It's ironic that some well-known start-ups that began as a David fighting a Goliath over time themselves became Goliath and susceptible to attack by smaller Davids. Bo Burlingham wrote an inspiring book back in 2005, *Small Giants: Companies that Choose to be Great Instead of Big*,[6] and it documents various stories of small companies that chose greatness over bigness. It's a thought-provoking read and reminds us that size is certainly not everything. Abi and I took that to heart, and like many others chose to aim for greatness not size. Time will tell how successful we are. But it was a conscious decision.

---

[5] The original David and Goliath story can be found in the Bible in the book I Kings 17, although today the more secular meaning is that of an underdog situation in which a smaller, weaker opponent faces a bigger, stronger adversary.

[6] Bo Burlingham, *Small Giants: Companies that Choose to be Great Instead of Big*, London, Portfolio, 2005.

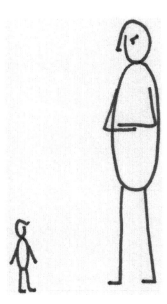

Fig. 13.1   David and Goliath

When you have big vision but are too small to compete with the major multinationals, when you can't afford to hire an army of highly paid experts, when it becomes more about stewardship than ownership or appropriation of resources, then small enterprises such as The Conscious Project have to rely on thinking and agility, and it's ideas like a redefined virtual guild that will enable us to come out fighting—and give us a chance of success.

New Models and Next Steps for the Virtual Guild?

The notion of the guild continues to evolve and inspire and will continue to do so. I'm not sure whether Guy Watson at Riverford Farm[7] would describe what he does as a guild but the way Riverford has connected organic farmers and growers around the UK to work with an extensive network of local representatives[8] embodies the principles of conscious

[7] http://www.riverford.co.uk/enf/aboutus (accessed October 1, 2015).
[8] http://www.riverford.co.uk/enf/aboutus/franchise-with-riverford (accessed October 1, 2015).

collaboration through franchising. Franchising may be a dirty word for some, so it's important to identify what makes the Riverford example so interesting: in essence it's the principles of a shared concern for excellence, care and stewardship of the planet and its natural resources, and a desire to create a connection between people and farms and reduce inequality. Similarly international platforms such as Avaaz.org, change.org and national platforms such as 38Degrees.org.uk offer a way for individuals to consciously collaborate and campaign, with the aim of bringing about change and better outcomes for society.

We've already highlighted the example of the Start Network[9]—a platform for INGO collaboration and humanitarian reform, and the Humanitarian Leadership Academy,[10] both initiatives that although heavily contingent on their ability to secure sufficient funding are nonetheless ambitious in their vision and reliant on conscious collaboration to achieve their goals.

There are other iterations of the guild concept such as the Silicon Guild[11] in the Bay Area on the west coast of America. Formally launched in 2014, the silicon guild '…focuses on developing systems, tools, technologies, and live events to connect authors, leaders, and readers…' and is a 'convener of thought leadership.'[12]

And then there are individuals like John Willshire at Smithery.co who we met through another kind of virtual guild—the Do Lectures,[13] and with whom we have begun to collaborate—people who are redefining consultancy and innovation.

Digital Underpinnings

One thing that unites all of the virtual guild examples mentioned here is their reliance on technology as a way of connecting community and enabling conscious collaboration between members. Hardly a day goes

---

[9] www.startnetwork.org (accessed October 1, 2015).

[10] http://www.humanitarianleadershipacademy.org (accessed October 1, 2015).

[11] http://www.siliconguild.com (accessed October 1, 2015).

[12] http://www.siliconguild.com/about/ (accessed October 20, 2015).

[13] http://thedolectures.com (accessed October 1, 2015).

by without a new app or suite of collaboration software being launched, and these have revolutionized the way knowledge and other outputs are created and shared. Many of the apps provide a platform for conscious collaboration, enabling collaboration to scale, partnerships to expand, engagement to increase and facilitating the expansion of networks and communities.

I have a concern, however, that our heavy reliance on this digital architecture limits our opportunities for conscious collaboration in places where the electricity supply is unreliable, internet access and connectivity is limited/intermittent, and bandwidth is expensive/restricted or both. At the time of writing it is clear that there is real inequality across the globe in terms of internet access, and I fear this could compromise our ambition to consciously collaborate on the big issues and challenges of our time. Many organizations identify digital exclusion as a key risk and we need to be mindful of this and its impact on conscious collaboration. By relying on the web and its ability to enable easy virtual networking, we may be excluding the very voices we seek to consciously include—typically the elderly, women, children, marginalized communities and the poor. I don't know what the answer is, other than to continue to work to reduce this inequality by improving access and connectivity, and by ensuring that we continue to use a blended approach when collaborating and thus hear the quiet voices, and analogue channels and face-to-face human interaction. We also have a responsibility to actively seek ways of expanding our guild and ensuring our edges remain porous—that way we can play our part in unleashing the expertise and experience of these 'unusual suspects'.

In Summary

The traditional concept of the guild is a helpful starting point but it needs redefining in order to suit the aims of conscious collaboration. Virtual guilds offer a way of connecting conscious collaborators across industries and professions and uniting them around a common purpose, and where the aim of the virtual guild is to achieve positive social change, we see a way of to tackle some of the intractable issues of our day.

Virtual guilds offer a way for the underdog to tackle bigger, better-resourced operations and the digital underpinnings mean that virtual guilds are able to operate cost-effectively and nimbly, spanning a wide geography and reaching large networks and communities. The concept will continue to evolve and social business models will continue to adapt and incorporate the noble principles of the guild in order to achieve positive outcomes for our world.

Networks, platforms and social businesses such as The Conscious Project are already operating in the form of a virtual guild and the potential is vast. We need to be vigilant as we develop the virtual guild model to ensure transparency and openness, and avoid being closed or nepotistic, that is to say perpetuating the anachronistic model of the 'old boys' network'.[14] For that reason, even the virtual guild must have a literal and tangible dimension and use a blend of methods and approaches to ensure conscious collaboration retains its diversity and embraces difference, or else it risks losing one of its most important defining characteristics.

For Reflection

As you think about the concept of the virtual guild, why not take a few moments to reflect:

- What expertise could you bring to a virtual guild?
- Who would be in your virtual guild?
- Which skills, crafts, expertise or knowledge would you invite to your guild to ensure it extends its diversity?

---

[14] https://en.wikipedia.org/wiki/Old_boy_network (accessed October 20, 2015).

Part III

Action

Part III is about action. If you've found yourself challenged by what you've read so far, or nodding as you read some of the ideas, then sooner or later, you'll want to bring your conscious collaboration to life. Or perhaps you're already hard at work, rethinking partnerships and consciously collaborating, for good. Either way, what do we do next?

In this part we will remind ourselves of the importance of leadership, and some of the core leadership behaviors required for conscious collaboration now and further into the future. We will also reflect on how and where conscious collaboration happens, how we recognize it, and what we can do to encourage and enable it, before pulling the various strands together in conclusion.

14

Leadership

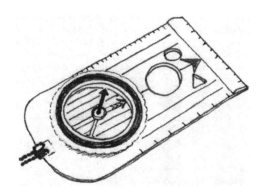

© The Editor(s) (if applicable) and The Author(s) 2016
B. Emmens, *Conscious Collaboration*,
DOI 10.1057/978-1-137-53805-5_14

Introduction

If there's one thing we've identified as we've explored conscious collaboration, it's that a unique type of leadership is required in order to make it happen. The demands and expectations of partners and the inclusive, generous, humble approach required leave little room for adherents to the traditional model of heroic leader, in which one individual grips the power and responsibility on behalf of the team and relies on insensitive displays of power and the reinforcing hierarchical structures to maintain the unequal status quo.

Conscious collaboration does not suit leaders with big egos or those who are keen to protect their own interests. But how do we spot the behaviors that can derail collaboration, and conversely, how can we nurture the leadership behaviors that lead to collaborative success? This chapter takes the competencies we identified in Chap. 6 and goes further, identifying some of the leadership behaviors which are central to conscious collaboration and its success.

In Chap. 6 I suggested the core competencies which I consider to be an absolute given; these competencies can also be described as leadership competencies. To recap, they cover the following five areas:

- Listening and dialogue—*actively listen to different perspectives; establish and maintain clear communication and dialogue.*
- Working with others—*establish clear objectives; actively participate and contribute positively to achieve collaboration objectives; share useful information and knowledge; challenge decisions and behavior that contradict values and/or collaboration objectives; foster inclusive, collaborative, transparent and accountable relationships; use negotiation and conflict resolution skills to support positive outcomes.*
- Self-awareness—*demonstrate understanding of your skills and how they complement those of others; show awareness of your own strengths and limitations and their impact on others; seek and reflect on feedback to improve your performance.*
- Critical judgment—*demonstrate initiative and suggest creative improvements; demonstrate tenacity to achieve results; exercise judgment in challenging situations in the absence of specific guidance.*

- Motivating and influencing others—*inspire others by clearly articulating and demonstrating the values, core purpose and principles that underpin the collaboration; inspire confidence in others; provide regular and ongoing informal and formal feedback; recognize the contribution of others; adapt leadership style to the time frame and changing situation.*

In addition, in Chaps. 7 and 8 we looked closely at the values of generosity, humility and stewardship, and I suggested they are core values for anyone involved in conscious collaboration—leaders included.

We know that leadership is fundamentally important—both in terms of setting the tone and in terms of actually modeling collaborative behaviors. But what kind of leadership? I suggest it's leadership that is both distributed and courageous.

Distributed?

Distributed leadership takes the focus away from the characteristics of an individual leader or situationally specific aspects, and instead looks at how leadership happens between people and in the context of a complex organization or system. As a model, it is especially salient when we look at tasks that are distributed across an organization, as it focuses on leadership as a social process at the intersection of leaders, followers, the situation and the task itself, and it implies that every single individual involved in the collaboration has a responsibility to demonstrate leadership behaviors.

In collaboration, particularly in the aid sector, there often an expectation that a leader will come up with the ideas and framework for collaboration, and play a key role in problem solving and coming up with answers and action plans. There are times when there is little scope for participation in the collaborative process, and the organization tends to be run like a machine or an engine, that is to say a series of inputs are made according to a pre-planned formula or project plan, the organization does the work, and the outputs are delivered. Historically there has rarely been much sense of the aid system being a complex adaptive system—instead, technocratic approaches have tended to be preferred, giving little space for individual autonomy and participation in planning, delivery and decision making processes.

Courageous?

By courageous I mean the type of leadership that doesn't shy away from the difficult conversations that need to be had, or from giving feedback. The type of leadership that acknowledges disagreement and dissonance when it arises and mediates conflict fairly, working toward reconciliation wherever possible. I mean the type of leadership that embraces diversity, ambiguity and the unknown, and is not afraid to say 'I don't know, let's find out'. The type of leadership that isn't afraid to act on well-informed intuition or to intervene and redirect when needed. The type of leadership that is comfortable with 'gaps'; the moments of silence which arise when colleagues are in deep thought or reflection.

Technical Competencies

I suggested in Chap. 6 that technical competencies for those involved in collaboration were becoming increasingly important; my own experience is that those of us that have or share the responsibility for leading, facilitating or brokering conscious collaboration do require certain technical competencies.

The first of these areas is digital literacy,[1] that is to say the knowledge skills and behaviors associated with the use of digital devices such as smartphones, tablets, laptops, desktop computers and their output, as well as relating to the data itself. I've mentioned the plethora of platforms and apps that exist to enable effective collaboration—in many contexts this has become routine and being able to use them confidently is expected. Also expected as routine are the knowledge, skills and expertise—the competencies—to build mini-websites, moderate online

---

[1] https://en.wikipedia.org/wiki/Digital_literacy (accessed October 18, 2015).

communities, handle inputs and data from discussions or jams, record and publish content (often while on the move), create interactive documents, engage in blogging and the use of social media. Being competent in such things in this hyperconnected age is an important enabler of the collaboration itself and ensuring the desired outcomes are achieved, but competence, even mastery, is equally important in order to be able to tell the collaboration story afterwards.

Three other areas of technical competence I would highlight as being important include:

* Artistic creativity, in the sense of being able to design and communicate creative processes and artistically convey inputs and collaboration conversations through graphical or visual note-taking. There are experts you can hire of course, and I've certainly been inspired by the work of Endless Possibilities,[2] whose artistic expertise has transformed collaborations I've been supporting between nonprofit organizations. But these are skills that we as facilitators should be developing.
* Coaching approach, including an understanding of different coaching models for individuals and groups, neurolinguistic programming (NLP), human behavior and psychology, mediation and conflict resolution.
* Intercultural fluency, that is to say experience of living and/or regularly working in different cultural contexts together with a deep understanding of and familiarity with local history, cultural norms and practices.

The Starting Point for Conscious Collaboration

Although theoretically anyone can initiate conscious collaboration, the reality is that it is often those in management or leadership roles who have an opportunity to do so. Such roles afford, generally, more autonomy and allow for different perspectives on the business or operations themselves, as well as a clearer sense of what is happening in the wider

---

[2] http://endlesspossibilities.eu (accessed October 18, 2015).

external environment. Professionally qualified managers and leaders may also have ready access—through a professional association or institution—to external networks and stakeholders.

Many of the collaborations I've been involved with, and plenty that I observe, have been catalyzed by an awakening to a live issue or an impending crisis. Conscious collaborations typically emerge from informal conversations between leaders—perhaps in a bar or as a side-meeting at a conference or summit—before moving to a modest space, perhaps a couple of desks in the corner of someone's office, or a garage…

There is a lot which mitigates our ability to keep our eyes open to collaborative potential, but it is nonetheless a discipline we should practice diligently. Collaborative possibilities can emerge from seemingly insignificant connections or conversations; for those openings to happen for us, we need to be practiced at initiating open dialogue, whether we tend to be introverted or extroverted. Open dialogue is characterized by powerful open questions—why, what, where, when, who, how—and we need to have the humility to answer 'I don't know, how can we find out?' For serendipitous moments to happen regularly, we need to work on removing the chance and make a habit of getting out more, and fire-starting conversations. This is also a good way of ensuring that when we collaborate we are open to collaborating with someone new, for as we have highlighted already, one of the potential risks in collaboration is to only collaborate within closed networks which lack diversity and the degree of difference or friction that can lead to much more robust and sustainable outcomes.

Brokering Collaboration

Based on the potent combination of intuition, insight and experience, some people develop the skill of collaboration brokering. These leaders play a special role in catalyzing and/or sponsoring conscious collaboration by effecting the right introductions and then stepping back and watching the connection blossom into collaboration. They may offer further input or guidance in terms of steering, but more often than not if you find someone playing the role of collaboration broker they are often happy to have given the collaboration a kick-start and will be entirely satisfied with playing no further role, other than to celebrate the positive outcome when the work is done!

Fig. 14.1   Find your brokers

It takes wisdom and humility to broker a conscious collaboration, and if you can find someone who is able to play this role and fits the description, then you have a head start over the rest!

Collaboration Killers

We considered when to exit a collaboration in Chap. 4—and knowing when to call time, for yourself or your organization, or the collaboration itself—is an important skill. For our own part though, we need to acknowledge that there are certain actions or behaviors that crush the collaborative spirit and can even kill the collaboration.

Aside from unexpected and dramatic events—for example the untimely death of a key partner in the collaboration, or deliberate deception or sabotage—the biggest risk to conscious collaboration is from uncollaborative behaviors or actions that contradict the shared values or mindset. Logically these are the negative or contraindicators of the competencies I have highlighted earlier in the chapter. There are a couple of behaviors I'm talking about that are particularly worrisome:

- A scarcity mindset—the hallmarks of a scarcity mindset are centered around 'lack', and 'can do' attitudes become 'can't do'. Collaborators may have lost faith in the partnership or its objectives or consider the proposed outcomes to be out of reach. Perhaps a partner stops accepting the contribution or expertise of others as a gift and becomes increasingly self-sufficient and guarded with existing resources, without looking outwards for new resources. A scarcity mindset saps the energy and enthusiasm of a collaboration over time. Although it can be hard to pinpoint in the early stages it is so toxic that it is essential to call it out as soon as you sense it! Any action or intervention required must be fair and proportionate, but decisive.

• Greed, selfishness or self-interest—this may become evident when a partner covertly appropriates or accumulates resources for themselves or their organization, makes decisions that favor their organization or contrives to use the decision-making processes and the group to advance their own position or status within the collaboration. As with the scarcity mindset, greed, selfishness or self-interest can be masked and are not always easy to spot in the early stages of collaboration. However, they are toxic behaviors and where there is evidence then swift action must be taken to ensure the collaboration survives.

Co-creating Your Collaboration Competencies

It can be of huge value to a collaboration if time is invested to co-create a simple suite of competencies—in other words behaviors—at an early stage. Collaboration partners can then use these to hold one another to account as well as to ease the selection and induction/onboarding of new partners. I admit that defining competencies isn't always an exciting task or even an easy task—some familiarity with competency frameworks may be useful. Resources permitting, it is something that can be done very effectively with the support of an external facilitator and I would advocate this wherever possible as it enables collaboration partners to participate fully in shaping the culture and working practices.

When Sara Swords and I worked with Action Aid to lead the development of the core humanitarian competencies framework that I referred to in Chap. 6, we were sure to invest time with the representatives and participants from the 19 INGOs that comprised the consortium up front, so there was no doubt about what was expected during the process in terms of collaborative behaviors. But before that we also chose to invest time as facilitators and collaboration partners—that is Sara, Jonathan,

Bijay, myself and a couple of Bijay's colleagues at Action Aid. Why did we do that? Well, we were about to head into an incredibly ambitious and intense process that would attempt something that had not been done before. In addition, resources (time and money) were finite—as organizations we hadn't worked that closely together, and given the public funds and importance of the process we were going to be subject to a great deal of scrutiny—so we needed to know that we had something that could guide us as the pressure increased and in the event that tempers became frayed or upset was caused. The fact that it was a fruitful collaboration and we didn't have to intervene as a result of conflict or a breakdown in relationship/s is something I attribute to this foundational work—investment up front.

No Smoothing

I referred to 'smoothing' in Chap. 2—where a facilitator or broker falls into the trap of 'smoothing' over difference or conflict. In a word—'Don't!' As Jesse Lyn Stoner at the Seapoint Center for Collaborative Leadership says when writing about situational team decision making: 'Collaboration does not require consensus!'[3]

Recognizing when smoothing is at risk of happening, or when you yourself are more at risk of smoothing disagreement or conflict, is a vital skill for those with leadership responsibilities. In many ways, each individual in the collaboration has a responsibility to be aware of the risks and to avoid smoothing behaviors, and we are accountable to each other in that regard.

I have had to learn about the consequences of smoothing the hard way, and I am still learning—it comes harder to some of us I guess! Like many, I tend to prefer harmony over discord, and do not generally seek confrontation or conflict. But there are times when, as we have seen—particularly in the context of collaboration—difference must be invited and celebrated. An abundance mindset sees potential in all options, and this approach is what leaders must nurture in themselves and others.

---

[3] http://seapointcenter.com/situational-team-decision-making/ (accessed October 20, 2015).

The impact of differences and disagreements between collaboration partners are greatly mitigated by a clear vision and a clear set of outcomes which partners are often able to realign with, once the constructive debate has taken place. Leaders therefore play an important role in negotiating space for constructive debate, in setting the tone of the debate and in reminding those working together why they came together in the first place.

Conscious Collaborators

When I took few moments to bring to mind leaders who I think personify conscious collaboration, and who embody many of the attributes, competencies and skills we have considered in this chapter, the result surprised me. Rather than recalling well-known public names that regularly appear in the media (which is what I'd anticipated would happen) the names that immediately came to mind were people like you and me, who along with their delightful idiosyncrasies (we all have them) are people that are making courageous decisions and doing extraordinary things, often with no guarantee of success. Individuals who demonstrate, in my judgment at least, great tenacity, vision and humility in their collaborative endeavors. I thought of Caroline Hotham and the role she played in bringing the Context Project to life,[4] and who at the time of writing manages the innovative Start Fund,[5] and Sean Lowrie, who at the time of writing directs the Start Network.[6] I thought of Ros Tennyson at the Partnership Brokers Association,[7] and the work she has done to establish partnership brokering as a recognized profession. I thought of Jim Prouty, and his leading role in creating SAFR,[8] the first global fund of its kind to support ethical banking models. I thought of Lynda Gratton and her commitment to collaborative research through consortia such as the Hot Spots Movement's Future of Work initiative.[9] I thought of

[4] http://contextproject.org (accessed October 18, 2015).
[5] http://www.startnetwork.org/start-fund (accessed October 18, 2015).
[6] www.startnetwork.org (accessed October 18, 2015).
[7] http://partnershipbrokers.org (accessed October 18, 2015).
[8] http://sfre.bluinc.co.uk (accessed October 18, 2015).
[9] http://www.hotspotsmovement.com/research-institute.html (accessed October 18, 2015).

Ted Lankester, co-founder of the Community Health Global Network,[10] which networks communities around the world and supports them in their quest to transform their own health, well-being and development. And there are many other men and women who are redefining the way we work together, for good.

In Summary

Leaders have it within their power to make or break conscious collaboration, whether through their actions, behavior or the tone they set. We all have a responsibility to model leadership behaviors that enable collaborative expression and activity, and they include being courageous, humble and decisive.

Essential leadership behaviors can be grouped under five areas: listening and dialogue, working with others, self-awareness, critical judgment and motivating and influencing others. Specifically, I would highlight the following behaviors:

- actively listening, actively participating and contributing, challenging decisions and behaviors that contradict the values, foster inclusive, collaborative, transparent and accountable relationships, show awareness of strengths and limitations and their impact, seek and reflect feedback, demonstrate initiative and tenacity and exercise judgment, provide regular and ongoing feedback and recognize the contribution of others.

New leadership competencies for those involved in leading, facilitating or brokering collaboration are required, and I've suggested they fall primarily under four areas: digital literacy, artistic creativity, coaching approach and intercultural fluency.

The collaborative spirit can be crushed where there is a scarcity mindset among one or more of the collaboration partners, or when greed, selfishness or self-interest become apparent. To mitigate the risk of this arising,

---

[10] http://www.chgn.org (accessed October 18, 2015).

it is well worth investing time at the outset in defining competencies—that is the core collaborative behaviors you want to see. As well as providing a behavioral framework for the collaboration, such a process often contributes to the building of trust between collaboration partners.

It's also important for differences to be able to surface constructively during collaboration and leaders must demonstrate self-awareness at such moments and avoid seeking to smooth over disagreements. This requires courage and strength to hold the space for negotiation and debate, and ultimately reconciliation if required.

Finally, in the examples of conscious collaborators that I briefly highlight above, I infer that anyone (and everyone) has the potential to collaborate consciously—it's a choice we can make. It entails modeling a set of collaborative (leadership) behaviors and the result is to inspire those who work with them, and ultimately to do good.

For Reflection

As you think about the implications of conscious collaboration for leadership, and critical leadership behaviors, why not take a few moments to reflect:

- What is your preferred leadership style when collaborating?
- Which leadership behaviors could you develop further, in order to collaborate more consciously and more effectively?
- Where are there opportunities for you to demonstrate leadership in collaboration?
- How can you help create a culture of distributed leadership in partnerships where you are involved, or that you oversee?

15

Principles and Processes

Introduction

Early on in the book I presented the collaboration continuum—a model that situated collaboration as a choice and a state which should be considered neither better nor worse than the other states in the model, and once again I acknowledge the work of Jesse Lyn Stoner at the Seapoint Center

© The Editor(s) (if applicable) and The Author(s) 2016   **175**
B. Emmens, *Conscious Collaboration*,
DOI 10.1057/978-1-137-53805-5_15

for Collaborative Leadership[1] and Dion Hinchcliffe[2] for being catalysts for my own thinking about conscious collaboration.

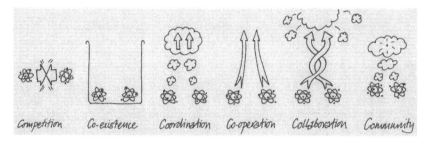

Fig. 15.1   The collaboration continuum

The model identifies various distinct states which describe the nature of the relationship and the way we work together; each state may be legitimate at various stages in a project cycle, for example whether scoping and planning or implementing or evaluating.

Recognizing which state we *are* in with regard to our working relationships, and which state we need to *be* in, is important for many reasons as it influences, for example, the choice of business model, the design of the business processes and the implementation of operating protocols. It is especially important, however, for ensuring clarity with regard to roles and responsibilities within the relationship, and individual behaviors.

Recognizing Where We Are at on the Continuum

I think it's helpful to briefly consider the characteristics of the main states as that will help us identify where we and/or our organizations are at in terms of working with others, and gain a better understanding of the nature of our relationship.

---

[1] http://www.seapointcenter.com (accessed October 20, 2015).
[2] http://www.dionhinchcliffe.com (accessed October 20, 2015).

- Competition—Individuals or organizations in competition tend to compete head to head on an issue (for example, product, price, quality) or look for gaps in the market and then adapt their offer accordingly. In the airline industry we see competitive collaboration in the form of multi-carrier alliances in response to market changes and pressures. In the aid sector we see INGOs that ordinarily compete for funding choose to collaborate in certain areas including advocacy and campaigning or programming, while remaining in competition in other areas.

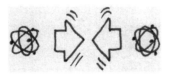

Fig. 15.2 Competition

- Co-existence—Individuals and organizations that co-exist may appear indifferent or laissez-faire in their attitudes toward each other and typically do their own thing for their own stakeholders, neither competing nor co-ordinating. Co-existing organizations may duplicate each other but their loyal customer or stakeholder base means they don't see the need to compete or fight for market share. Organizations may co-exist for many years, in reality keeping a watchful eye on each other and emerging threats.

Fig. 15.3 Co-existence

- Co-ordination—Individuals and organizations that co-ordinate typically have shared interests and multiple communication channels; they have a working understanding that enables them to get along and minimize duplication, but incentives to co-operate may be lacking or inadequate and interaction may tend to be more transactional. Self-co-ordination mechanisms exist in the form of voluntary associations or networks, but in many cases co-ordination is undertaken by an external regulator or formal, sometimes statutory co-ordination mechanism. In the aid sector, particularly in emergency response situations, it is the United Nations Office for the Co-ordination of Humanitarian Affairs that has the mandate to co-ordinate INGO activity.

Fig. 15.4 Co-ordination

- Co-operation—Individuals or organizations that are co-operating have typically made a conscious decision to do that as at least some of their desired outcomes overlap or coincide, and/or they have a common interests or stakeholders. Co-operation may involve sharing of resources—often proportional to the organization's means—and/or a degree of interoperability in the form of common processes or protocols and/or some shared operating procedures. Mutual trust tends to be higher than in a co-ordination relationship, as does interaccountability. When resources are scarce or risk needs to be spread, organizations might choose to co-operate and ultimately share the benefit or success.

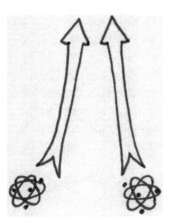

Fig. 15.5 Co-operation

- Collaboration—Individuals or organizations that are collaborating have also (usually) made a conscious decision to do so in order to real-ize a shared vision and set of outcomes which they are not capable of achieving on their own, whether due to lack of resources, competen-cies, capacities or the scale and complexity of the challenge being tack-led. Conscious collaboration is typically characterized by equitable participation and requires high trust and a high level of interaccount-ability. Values, systems and processes are ideally co-designed and co-created by the partners as part of the collaboration itself, and in some cases, organizations that are in a collaboration choose to merge or inte-grate their collaborative activities to create a new entity.

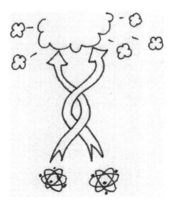

Fig. 15.6 Collaboration

- Community—Community is the state that can arise post-collaborative activity when a collaboration has taken on its own form and identity, and may even become a new entity with its own values, systems and processes. Well-functioning communities typically have a deeply embedded sense of identity and purpose, and continue to evolve and co-create new systems and processes. A community is often able to secure high levels of engagement and greater levels of discretionary effort and behavior than a collaboration.

Fig. 15.7   Community

Choosing to Collaborate

At the outset I indicated a few drivers for collaboration and these included the nature, scale or complexity of the challenge being faced and recognition of a lack of resources, capacity or expertise in an organization. Choosing to collaborate is an entirely appropriate response where something new needs to be created by way of response or intervention or a radical shift or change is required, which simply cannot be achieved by a single entity. But with collaboration comes certain responsibilities and it is by no means the easy option.

In general, the more to the right of the continuum model individuals or organizations find themselves, the greater the commitment, time, resources, accountability, communications and formality (legal agreements)—and the lower the autonomy. Toward the left of the continuum model, autonomy increases and commitment, accountability and formality decrease. Time, resources and communications can still be fairly high, even for the states toward the left of the continuum.

Choosing where you want to be, in a transparent, participatory way, is imperative—and not making a choice is nonetheless a choice, and will leave you at the mercy of others.

Principled Collaboration

As we've seen, collaboration works well where there are shared values—typically co-created ones—and when there are clear principles to guide the collaborative activity and the behaviors of those involved in the collaboration. I made reference to 'operating principles' earlier in the book, and while these can be integrated with a 'collaboration agreement', they can make a specific contribution of their own.

Operating principles do not need to be lengthy or elaborate, but they do need to be authentic and must avoid being superficial or trite. That is a fine line to tread, but what I mean is that simply saying: '*We agree to respect each other*' isn't really sufficient or even that helpful when it comes to applying the principles. I suggest it's more helpful to set out briefly how collaboration partners will deal with a complaint, or a disagreement, or a concern, and then to describe a simple process, and the behaviors that are expected from those who respond. For example, something like this could be much more helpful:

> We are committed to this collaboration, and to working inclusively and respectfully in order to achieve the outcomes described […]. However, we recognize that in the heat of the moment either or both of us might make a mistake, jump to a hasty conclusion or inadvertently cause upset or offense. If during the course of our collaboration that happens, or either party has a concern about anything the other party has done, then after a

quick sense check by the party with the concerns, a careful conversation between senior staff in both organizations should take place at the earliest opportunity. The conversation should be face to face if possible, or by phone, and the concerns presented calmly and objectively, with the other party/parties being given an opportunity to respond. For as long as we're collaborating, our mutual intent is that to work toward a reconciliation in the interests of our vision and desired outcomes.

In my experience a few bullet points covering the shared values and core behaviors, together with two or three brief paragraphs like the one above—to cover, for example, how the collaboration might deal with an injection of resources (money) or a lack of money, how disagreements will be dealt with, and how decisions will be made—is sufficient. I've rarely needed more than a single page, two at most. On occasions the principles also include a brief note on how the collaboration would be terminated if necessary. The purpose of the operating principles is to provide a simple guide for how to deal with common collaboration issues and to ensure the collaborative intent and spirit is not lost over something that is resolvable.

Collaboration Agreements

In any collaboration, a collaboration agreement is vital. My experience is that some collaborations can carry on for a long time without much in the way of formal or legal agreement, but when an unexpected issue arises, they are crucial. A crisis point is not the moment to begin drafting or renegotiating a collaboration agreement and indeed, having one already in place could very well be what saves the collaboration from implosion or disintegration.

Most collaboration experts would advocate a co-created collaboration agreement rather than one that is imposed by one or other of the partners, and the collaboration agreement typically acts as an overarching Memorandum of Understanding. Collaboration agreements can be simple and straightforward, or more complex, depending on the financial or reputational risk associated with the collaboration and whether lawyers need to be involved. Again, having worked with some organizations that insist on layer upon layer of agreement and contract and multiple governance mechanisms, my conclusion is the simpler the collaboration agreement, the better, and it is worth insisting on this wherever possible! It's also quite usual for specific activities to have their own separate (legal) agreement or contract, especially if resources are involved or being invested, and these will vary according to the partners involved and their protocols.

At its best a collaboration agreement is a statement of intent as well as practice—it deals with the fundamental questions: who, why, what, where, when and how, as well as the 'what if?'. The primary purpose is to clarify who is involved, the purpose of the collaboration, how it will work and what it will entail, the intended outcomes and the timeline and how communications will be handled. It can also contain specific elements such as dealing with disagreements or grievances, how new partners can join, or existing partners leave and how the collaboration will be terminated. A brief checklist below highlights a few suggested headings:

Basic Checklist for a Collaboration Agreement

- Who is involved? Who are the representatives?
- Purpose of the collaboration? Vision? Intended outcomes?
- Scope of the collaboration? Collaboration activities? Resources required? Success indicators? Key relationships and anticipated responsibilities?
- Timeline? Key milestones?
- Protocols? Values? Operating principles? Decision-making process? Governance and accountability? Risk management? Financial arrangements, including funding?
- Review process?
- Communication protocols—internal and external? Branding? Intellectual property and copyright?
- Process for dealing with disagreements, complaints or grievances?
- Joining procedure? Exit procedure? Termination?

A wide range of resources including templates for a collaboration agreement are available from organizations such as the Partnership Brokers Association[3] or the Partnering Initiative.[4]

Brokering and Facilitation

I've mentioned brokering and facilitation a few times as a role that needs to be played in a collaboration. In reality it is primarily the partners within the collaboration who will need to play the different roles that are required at different points in a collaboration, although from time to time—though rarely all the time—there may be external support in the form of a broker, convenor or facilitator. The different roles in the collaboration will depend on the stage the collaboration is at, and what is required at that stage. The roles might typically include, to name but a few:

- Mobilizing or bringing together stakeholders
- Mapping resources
- Brokering conversations and dialogue
- Negotiating space for discussion or reflection
- Facilitating a jam
- Critically reflecting on progress or otherwise
- Challenging behaviors or decisions
- Mediating in conflict situations
- Identifying emerging issues or opportunities
- Facilitating activities and implementation
- Facilitating action learning or thinking processes
- Facilitating evaluation and review processes

Facilitating conscious collaboration requires 'conscious facilitation'! It needs dexterity and flexibility, together with many of the competencies identified in Chaps. 6 and 14. Facilitation may need to be tight or loose—in other words clearly mapped processes when, for example,

---

[3] http://www.partnershipbrokers.org (accessed October 20, 2015).
[4] http://www.thepartneringinitiative.org (accessed October 20, 2015).

working against the clock to make a decision, or open, clear spaces with much less structure, for example when jamming and coming up with ideas, and of course anything in between, depending on what the collaboration and/or the individual partners need. And determining what the collaboration and/or individual partners need at any one point could be considered both an art and a science!

Conscious Reflection

Our capacity for introspection and willingness to learn more about ourselves and our purpose is an important component of collaboration. The individual exercise of conscious reflection is a discipline and takes practice, but as we saw in Chap. 8, when we considered 'accompaniment', there can be real value when the partners in the collaboration choose to consciously reflect on the collaboration at regular intervals. Drawing on my partnership broker training, I often encourage those involved in collaborations to take a few minutes at the beginning or the end of the day and to journal their thoughts and concerns in a small notebook. I suggest they try to keep this practice up for a period of a week or two, or even up to a month. It doesn't need very long—I'd say five minutes at most in one sitting, and I encourage people to use a timer—but over time it is a technique that helps the individual see patterns emerging—whether they may be patterns of behaviors, common concerns or issues or moments of breakthrough. The principle of conscious reflection and the discipline of journaling helps the individual learn and grow as a broker, and the insights they are then able to share (through a coaching or mentoring relationship) or indeed with colleagues in the collaboration have been very helpful.

In Summary

It's important to be able to identify which stage we *are* at in our working relationships, and which stage we need to *be* at, as this will have a bearing on the choices we make with regard to business model, business processes and the implementation of operating protocols. The collaboration continuum is a simple model that helps us do this, and identifies various characteristics of each state.

Collaboration is a choice, and not always appropriate. Equally there are times when organizations that have chosen to collaborate judge some individual activities to be outside the scope of the collaboration, and thus find that different parts of the organization are simultaneously at different stages on the continuum.

When working together in a collaboration, a co-created collaboration agreement is essential. This typically sets out the principles that will govern the collaboration and important details such as who is involved, why the collaboration exists and what outcomes it intends to achieve. Also covered are protocols that will guide activities, communications, how disagreements and grievances will be dealt with, how new partners will join, or existing partners can leave and the way in which the collaboration will be wound up or the circumstances under which it may be terminated.

Conscious facilitation of the collaboration is a shared responsibility although external support may be required or deemed necessary. Facilitators need to be flexible and able to assume a range of different roles according to what the collaboration or individual partners need at any given moment. And finally, for anyone involved in the collaboration, and whatever their role, the discipline of regular personal reflection (on any or all aspects of the collaboration) is to be commended, and will be invaluable when it comes to feedback, making adjustments and reviewing success.

For Reflection

As you think about the principles and processes associated with conscious collaboration, why not take a few moments to reflect:

* At which stage do you judge your organization's various relationships with other organizations to be, according to the collaboration continuum model? Why?
* Which principles guide your current collaborations?
* How would you describe your preferred facilitation style?
* What opportunities for growth are there for you as a conscious facilitator?

16

Micro-outcomes

© The Editor(s) (if applicable) and The Author(s) 2016
B. Emmens, *Conscious Collaboration*,
DOI 10.1057/978-1-137-53805-5_16

Introduction

Talk to anyone involved in a collaboration, whether as a partner or a facilitator, and your conversation will likely reveal just how hard collaboration can be. With luck, once you've heard about the collaboration woes and war stories, you might also get to hear about the moments of elation where perhaps a long-anticipated breakthrough emerged, or the about the camaraderie and sense of community and peer support that carried individuals through dark times.

Most collaboration journeys require a considerable investment of time and emotional energy, often more than is initially anticipated. Marking progress and achievements is an important ritual that can tangibly strengthen engagement and a sense of belonging. In this chapter we'll look at what constitutes progress and how achievements or successes could be celebrated. I'm going to refer to those achievements or successes as micro-outcomes as they are significant but small outcomes that mark progress toward the ultimate outcome.

For reference, we'll build on some of the ideas in Chap. 15 and look at the micro-outcomes that could be associated with the main stages of collaboration.

The Early Stages

I think it is the *time* that collaboration requires, especially in the early stages, that often takes people by surprise. The initial, exploratory discussions about collaborating are an important part of the process, but they may feel repetitive and can be exasperating! At times the initial stage of collaboration might seem like a surreal courtship ritual where nobody quite knows the 'rules', or it may just feel like a 'talking shop'. Often the conversations circle around and around until the point at which one or more of those present call a halt to the talk and initiates a call to action. Two things are certain though: each collaboration will have its unique characteristics, and they all need to go through this stage, whether quickly or slowly.

In and around the important small talk and side conversations that can help build rapport and establish trust in the initial stage of collaboration, the tangible process of collaborating is getting underway. It may be obvious in the energy, enthusiasm and ideas of individuals keen to channel their passion into co-creating a thing or bringing about a very necessary outcome, or it may be less obvious and tucked away in a series of cautious and sensitive interactions which venture ideas, offers and concerns.

In all this, it can be difficult to judge when a milestone has been reached, or what constitutes a micro-outcome. Getting to the point where the purpose of the collaboration is clear and can be easily articulated, as well having clarity on who is (and will be) involved, could certainly be considered a micro-outcome, and can be celebrated. To me, it's clear that this point has been reached when a draft purpose statement (why) has been agreed, partners are identified and on board (who), and key communication points have been drafted to assist the collaboration in announcing its intent to the wider world. These days a simple website or landing page on the internet can be very helpful to serve a tangible, credible artifact and spur the collaboration on to the next stage.

It's often in the initial stages that a draft collaboration agreement is sketched out by partners, and the process of co-creating the agreement is usually experienced as positive, reflecting the optimism that is percolating through the collaboration initiative.

Building Together

As the euphoria of deciding to collaborate wears off, a sense of being overwhelmed lurks in the shadows as the scale of the challenge, commitment and resources required begins to sink in. If the initial stages are akin to courtship and commitment, with the celebratory 'honeymoon', then this is the point where a different kind of work begins. It's possible for this next stage to drag, as substantial investments of time and energy are required in order to negotiate the shared values (how we're going to work together), the scope of work and how that work will be divided up. The aspirational collaboration agreement that provided the basis for proceeding now gets tested and refined—in real time! The negotiation and renegotiation can be demanding, and may even require vision and outcomes statements to be revised. External facilitation can be a real asset at this stage as partners storm and relationships strain. This is the point where concerns surface and need to be handled carefully and constructively.

Discussion about resources can be contentious at this stage, especially if new resources (including funding) will be required. Which partner will be responsible for the financial management and administration? What will happen if new intellectual property is created? Working through the details will sometimes be painful, and it's easy to lose sight of what the collaboration was all about in the first place.

Other than world-class negotiation skills, sound project or operations management expertise is an asset during this process and will help keep things on track. If those skills aren't present in the core collaboration team then the collaboration risks becoming unbalanced as work gets unevenly distributed to other parts of the partners' organizations. A project (collaboration) plan can be very helpful at this point to indicate the key milestones, which can be celebrated appropriately at intervals. The production of the final collaboration agreement, the collaboration plan and key milestones, a communications plan, a budget—these are all what I would consider to be micro-outcomes that demonstrate progress toward achieving the collaboration's vision and intended outcomes. It may feel unglamorous, but these are the essential components of collaboration. In many ways this is like being in the collaboration's engine room or the boiler house, in our overalls, paying attention to the machinery or the plumbing—it's fundamentally important work and often hidden from everyone's gaze.

The volume of work at this stage will be phenomenal, and resources will typically be quite limited. It's crucial that we don't overlook the need for leaders to model healthy working habits and this is the time to embed practices that help individuals avoid burnout and retain their enthusiasm for the collaboration. Giving recognition to individuals when and where it's due, ensuring incentives are aligned with the desired collaboration culture and reinforcing the shared values and operating principles are important priorities for those leading the collaboration.

The Work of the Collaboration

As the work of the collaboration gets under way in earnest, micro-outcomes may become further apart, depending on the collaboration's timeline. For instance, if the collaboration exists to create, pilot and launch a product, or achieve a significant behavioral change, then it will be a long game! Marking the milestones continues to be an important ritual even at this stage—whether in the form of regular evaluations and learning reviews, an annual gathering or the beginnings of a virtual community—and the occasions when the tribe gathers can be hugely energizing for partners in the collaboration, as well as the much wider stakeholder group.

Collaboration is often 'won or lost in the trenches'—in other words micro-outcomes depend on the sterling work that's done by those deep within the partnership and although a core team can help facilitate and guide the collaboration progress and retain a high-level view, the hard graft is often delegated to those with the more appropriate technical competencies and more people are mobilized. As this happens, there is a risk that the collaborative vision becomes diluted, and so some of the early rituals will need to be repeated for newcomers in order to build engagement with the collaboration and begin creating a sense of community.

The discipline of regular review and seeking constructive feedback requires commitment, but it's during the work of the collaboration that its value becomes clear. Whether as part of a monitoring or evaluation framework and prescheduled at key milestones, or a regular calendar-based review at set intervals, establishing touchpoints that enable questions to be asked and honestly answered is vital. It's not unheard of for such reviews to become 'junction moments' and play a part in redirecting collaborative activity and/or unlocking new resources. Again, these points may mark micro-outcomes and can be shared within the collaboration or more widely. Regular blog posts can show the world what's happening and where progress is being made.

I mentioned the discipline of journaling in Chap. 15. For those in leadership roles or with the responsibility of facilitating collaboration, making a habit of regular conscious reflection and journaling, however brief those sessions might be, will be an asset in terms of being able to look back and see where progress has been made and where the micro-outcomes are. What often becomes evident as you look back through journal notes is the slow shift in behaviors and the sometimes imperceptible progress toward the ultimate outcome. This evolution does not always have obvious micro-outcomes, and thus the perspective a journal can bring complements other inputs, and at an appropriate point can be shared with the collaboration partners by way of review and encouragement.

Evaluating in Real Time

Real-time evaluation is a concept that has been written about at length elsewhere, but for the purpose of this topic, there are a couple of useful principles that we can apply and which will assist us as we reflect on and review the progress of the collaboration. Real-time evaluation is commonplace in the aid sector as is a way of providing feedback to managers and implementers in real time (rather than waiting until the project has finished), in a participatory manner. The two key principles are that feedback is provided 'in real time' and in a 'participatory manner', and this is what is so incredibly important when collaborating.

We considered the importance of feedback in Chap. 6, and it's worth reiterating the importance here. The competence, that is the demonstrable ability, of all those working in the collaboration to be able to give (and receive) feedback cannot be stressed enough. It is vital, to the extent that it can be worthwhile investing in the development of those skills within the collaboration at an early stage. Nancy Kline's influential book, *Time to Think*,[1] provides challenge, stimulation and guidance for facilitators looking to improve feedback processes and enhance the quality of listening and conversation.

Frameworks for evaluating collaboration are still at a relatively early stage of development: consultancy firms have tended to pioneer their own proprietary approaches while in the world of partnership brokering both the Partnership Brokers Association and the Partnering Initiative offer conceptual frameworks for evaluating the partnership itself (that is, primarily the principles and processes), which can be of use, although these conceptual frameworks require adaptation should the *outcome* of the partnership also need evaluating (for example the product, service, impact or change).

---

[1] Nancy Kline, *Time to Think*, London, Ward Lock, 1999.

I was recently part of an international, multidisciplinary evaluation team that undertook an evaluation of a global, collaborative research for development program. The process reminded me how complicated such an evaluation can be. When evaluators are reviewing design systems, processes, incentives, structures, outputs and more, against criteria such as relevance, quality, participation, scale, legal frameworks, ethics, impact and sustainability, it takes a huge amount of time and resources, and can feel overwhelming.

As thinking around 'conscious collaboration' evolves, and the need to evaluate the *why*, the *what* and the *how* (and the relationship between them) in one process emerges, we can expect to see huge steps forward in evaluation approaches, techniques and the accompanying guidance.

Measuring and Valuing

I'm personally not convinced by the maxim 'if you can't measure it you can't manage it'. Conscious collaboration invites us to rethink how we evaluate success, and for me the social dimension is often best told through stories. Case studies that tell the story of change and that give insight to the lived and shared experience of collaboration can tell us a great deal and guide our decisions and choices about the future.

Clearly there is an important role for (quantitative) data as well, and this could be in the form of 360° feedback—the system or process by which individuals receive confidential, anonymous feedback from the people who work around them—on the individuals involved in the collaboration, as well as in the form of stakeholder engagement surveys that gather perspectives, opinions and experiences of internal and external stakeholders.

So bringing it together, what we choose to measure and value sends an important message. In a conscious collaboration we should anticipate the need to evaluate holistically, and include areas such as: purpose, values, behaviors, alignment, processes, stewardship of resources, return on expectation and/or investment, impact and outcomes.

Ultimately I believe that it is the balanced scorecard and assurance-based approaches[2] that offer the most effective way of evaluating the performance and outcomes of conscious collaboration, taking into account the social, financial and environmental performance and broader issues of sustainability and drawing on a diverse range of inputs, quantitative and qualitative, to inform any reporting.

The Canary...

In and among all the thinking, models and conceptual frameworks for evaluating outcomes and identifying micro-outcomes, I want to come back to the issue of individual responsibility.

A long time ago—before the technological advances of the late twentieth century and when the UK relied on coal for much of its energy—coal miners working deep underground would always take a canary with them down the mine. Why? Apparently canaries, being very small and having a very fast heart rate, would succumb to a lack of oxygen or poisonous fumes (methane or carbon monoxide) much more quickly than a human. This was potentially life-saving to the miners, as such an eventuality would alert them to imminent danger and theoretically give them sufficient time to escape from the mine.

Fig. 16.1 The canary!

[2] You can find out more about assurance standards, accountability and performance at http://www.accountability.org/standards/index.html (accessed October 20, 2015).

It strikes me that those of us who lead or facilitate conscious collaboration are often in the position of being the canary. We act as a sentinel, able to see and sense impending hazards, environmental hazards or potential difficulties that lie ahead for the collaboration and the partners, often some time before others in the collaboration are aware. How can this be? If we are working effectively and consciously, we will remain objective, scanning the horizon for threats, challenges and pitfalls, sensing and intuiting the health of the emerging collaboration and intervening sensitively to ensure equity of participation and contribution. We may not be literally saving the lives of those in the collaboration, but metaphorically, we may be saving the life of the collaboration and our individual responsibility to the collaboration is to be taken very seriously indeed.

In Summary

In conscious collaboration it's important to mark the milestones and micro-outcomes that are achieved along the collaboration journey, particularly in the early stages where the investment of time and resources required can feel overwhelming. Being able to do so requires sound project management expertise and a clear sense of the collaboration timeline.

Building the collaboration continues to require hard work and can leave collaboration partners feeling weary. It's at this stage that the difficult discussions about resources and allocation of responsibilities bubble up, perhaps requiring renegotiation of the collaboration agreement and the need to reaffirm the collaborative vision and desired outcome. In these circumstances it's easy to lose sight of the goal, and find yourself wondering what it is all about. Regular reviews and feedback, maintaining and repeating some of the early rituals when new partners and/or individuals come on board, together with healthy habits such as conscious reflection—for example through regular journaling—can be very valuable, and help mark progress and achievement.

Evaluating the collaboration can quickly become a cumbersome process and in the absence of succinct frameworks or evaluation tools, the principles of real-time evaluation, with its emphasis on feedback in real time and in a participatory manner, can be adopted and applied to a scope of evaluation that is most valuable for the collaboration itself and its key stakeholders.

The personal, individual responsibility of all those involved in the collaboration, particularly those leading, facilitating or brokering, to act as sentinels cannot be overemphasized. This entails scanning the horizon for threats, as well as sensing and intuiting the health of the emerging collaboration and intervening sensitively to ensure equity of participation and contribution.

For Reflection

As you think about conscious collaboration, take a few moments to reflect on the outcomes you seek from any collaboration that you are involved in:

- What micro-outcomes can you anticipate, and how will you mark them?
- How will you determine whether your conscious collaboration is achieving its purpose?

17

Conclusion

Writing a conclusion on the vast subject of conscious collaboration, which we've only just begun to describe, feels somehow premature. So perhaps we should see this conclusion as merely the end of the beginning. When we started The Conscious Project in 2012 we were slightly ahead of the game—now we are in the thick of it! And when we started this book project the notion of conscious business was only just beginning to gain traction, at least in Europe. But the surge in interest from around the world is a very good thing—diverse views, experiences, insights and models will help us refine our thinking and distill the essence of conscious collaboration. In time, conscious collaboration will be the only type of collaboration.

Which Type of Collaboration?

In Chap. 15 I presented a simple framework to help us identify the nature of our collaboration, and to determine whether in fact the way we work with others is a collaboration or some other form of relationship. This is perhaps one of the most important points in the whole book—that

© The Editor(s) (if applicable) and The Author(s) 2016   **197**
B. Emmens, *Conscious Collaboration*,
DOI 10.1057/978-1-137-53805-5_17

collaboration is a very specific undertaking with implications in terms of commitment, resources, business model, business processes and operating protocols. As I said in Chap. 15, choosing to collaborate is an entirely appropriate reaction where something new needs to be created by way of response or intervention, or where we need to see a radical shift or change which simply cannot be achieved by a single entity. But conscious collaboration brings with it certain responsibilities, and although it can be tremendously powerful in achieving impossible outcomes, it is not an easy option!

As we look around us today, we see many different ways of working together, different relationships, partnerships, contracting arrangements, collaborations. In fact we see plenty of relationships that are masquerading as collaboration, but, on closer inspection, they couldn't be further from the real thing. We need to get better at identifying collaboration opportunities, and become comfortable calling other ways of working together what they are, which may be a simple contract, or co-operation agreement or some form of co-ordination.

Collaboration can be one of the most exhilarating, creative, inspiring and exhausting things we can do in our working life and if we should choose to collaborate then we must be fully prepared to follow through and accept the responsibilities it places upon us, and be ready to meet the demands of the collaboration. Conscious collaboration at its best is a place where we see community and a deep sense of commitment, engagement and belonging.

Conscious Collaboration

What sets conscious collaboration apart from *ordinary* collaboration and other ways of working together is its unrelenting focus on purpose—that is, achieving positive social and environmental outcomes that so far have eluded us. At its simplest but most profound level, conscious collaboration is about rethinking the way we work together, for good.

And by 'for good', I mean that includes both the good of those involved in the conscious process of collaborating and also the sustained good of those who will be touched by the outcome of the collaboration.

Conscious collaboration requires a belief that it is entirely within our grasp to effect this change, to bring about a conscious revolution in the way we work and in the impact and outcomes of the work we do. And that belief is a prerequisite, for as Henry Ford is reputed to have said: 'whether you think you can, or you think you can't, you're right.'

Conscious collaboration is a journey of discovery, and just as every journey begins with the first step,[1] so we have gone back toward the beginning to consider why we even choose to collaborate in the first place and how we can collaborate consciously and successfully. This entailed considering some of the underpinning values and principles in depth, as well as reflecting on how and where collaboration happens and what it requires of us personally.

In this book, particularly in Chaps. 6–8, I've highlighted what I believe to be some of the most important values that underpin conscious collaboration—generosity, humility and accompaniment. I've also suggested a handful of core competencies (or behaviors) that should be recruited and/or developed and/or modeled by all individuals within the collaboration—listening and dialogue, working with others, self-awareness, critical judgment and motivating and influencing others. These complement the technical competencies that are also required in the collaboration team.

Seizing the Moment

Recognizing an opportunity to collaborate as it emerges is more of a learned behavior than it is a formulaic or scientific process. Knowing whether to collaborate (or not) is rarely straightforward, but there are ways we can help ourselves. In Chaps. 9 and 10 we looked in some detail at where opportunities often emerge—it's often at the edges, whether they be the edge of the inside or—in the case of the edge being porous— the outside. It takes a certain openness and set of behaviors, as well as considerable effort, to create those serendipitous moments in which collaborative conversations emerge, and the seed of a vision germinates.

---

[1] Attributed to Lao Tzu in the Laozi, written more than 2500 years ago.

Courage is important in the initial stages as the collaboration emerges, and when the territory is uncharted and the topography intimidating. Those moments call for a special kind of boldness, and an embracing of the risks that go hand in hand with an ambitious vision. There will always be risks, and it's inevitable that some of those risks will severely challenge the collaboration and potentially destroy it. That's how it is when we attempt to do something big, something that's worth doing. It will be hard and not everyone will support us. In fact there may be dissent from within, and 'friendly fire' might come close to killing the collaboration. There will be times when courage to say 'no' or to walk away from an opportunity will be needed. Be prepared!

Fig. 17.1   Time to press the bold button!

I also identified courage as an important attribute, particularly in the context of challenging constructively and in giving (and receiving) feedback. Courage to challenge behaviors that contradict the values or principles of collaboration will be needed, and Chap. 15 also highlights the importance of having in place a simple collaboration agreement that can guide any intervention that's required as a result of a disagreement, grievance or inappropriate behavior.

When it's clear that it's time to collaborate—rapport is growing, trust is growing, the vision is shared, the purpose and outcome clear, the values are aligned, the synergy between partners is fizzing—then that's the time to seize the moment! Enjoy the euphoric feeling as it can often evaporate quickly, and get yourself prepared to dig deep into your reserves of energy. Conscious collaboration requires stamina and patience, and intentional behaviors particularly relating to generosity and humility.

Tracking Progress

A collaboration's success can largely depend on its ability to generate and assimilate feedback on its performance, and this feedback should be gathered according to a range of indicators that would typically elaborated in the collaboration agreement. They should include the collaborative behaviors of partners and the ongoing validity of the vision and desired outcomes.

Individual competence in giving and receiving feedback is one of the most important competencies in a collaboration—and in my experience the ability to give constructive feedback objectively and sensitively is not widely distributed, particularly among those working for aid agencies. Feedback is a gift, and receiving it as such is an important mindset. The frameworks and practical suggestions presented in Chap. 6, intended to guide and improve the way we give and receive feedback, are a useful starting point if you think that this is an area in which you could do better in your collaboration.

Feedback on the collaboration's performance and achievements as a whole requires a more holistic approach than one that merely evaluates the activities and outputs. In Chap. 16 I presented real-time evaluation as a way of providing feedback to the collaboration's leaders, managers and implementers—in real time and in a participatory manner. The scope of any evaluation should extend to include the partnership or collaboration itself, and the extent to which the collaboration values and principles are lived out by partners, as well as the big questions about relevance and whether the original stated purpose and desired outcomes are right.

Measuring and Recognizing Success

To a large extent, it is the evaluation process which enables a collaboration to give account for—and report on—its performance and to demonstrate the return on expectation and/or investment. Various reporting frameworks exist to make this process easier and the evaluation findings more accessible for a diverse set of stakeholders, and one such way is through stories of impact, as the Partnership Brokers Association have done for the Start Network through two papers, 'Dealing with Paradox' and 'Power and Politics',[2] which I commend for their honesty and deep insight into collaboration in all its rawness.

Choosing an evaluation method and process that fits the culture of the collaboration while enabling an honest review of the ongoing act of conscious collaboration, its achievements and successes and its progress toward its ultimate outcome, is something that should be prioritized in the early stages of the collaboration, and should ideally be described in the collaboration agreement. Clarity on what constitutes an achievement or success, and other milestones—for example the accomplishment of specific activities or tasks, or examples of individual behavior that models the collaboration's values and principles—is helpful and these points serve as waymarkers on the collaboration journey. I strongly encourage collaboration partners to recognize and mark these moments in a culturally appropriate way, as doing so sends an important message about what is valued and what gets rewarded, and also serves to build trust and collegiality among collaboration partners.

Clear Voices

Wise entrepreneurs often encourage newcomers to be sure to surround themselves with other brilliant people in order to be successful. And I understand why: the energy, encouragement and inspiration gained from having brilliant people close by and taking an interest in what we're doing pushes us further in pursuit of excellence and affirms our belief that we

---

[2] First instalment http://www.start-network.org/wp-content/uploads/2014/01/Dealing-with-paradox.pdf and the second instalment http://www.start-network.org/wp-content/uploads/2015/03/Power-Politics.pdf (accessed October 20, 2015).

will be able to achieve impossible things. However, in conscious collaboration, it is the diversity of voices that contribute to the achievement of extraordinary outcomes, even though (as we have been reminded) there may be differences and disagreements along the way that require mediation and sensitive intervention by those facilitating the collaboration. The temptation to smooth over these moments of dissonance and discomfort will be enormous and beguiling! In the end though, it is the myriad and multicolor threads woven together over time that create the stunning tapestry that only existed previously in the mind of its creator/s.

Listening to the different voices, and hearing them clearly—especially the quieter voices—is paramount, but doing so requires us to hold back and *actively* listen. And the ability to do that comes from a deep, and perhaps unfashionable, humility, as well as generosity that expresses itself in thoughts as well as in words and actions.

Conscious Networks

Conscious collaboration can be a consuming affair—to the extent that when we become wrapped up with our own collaboration, we can lose sight of what's going on in the wider world. In a collaboration, leaders and those with leadership responsibilities are especially susceptible to feelings of isolation and loneliness as they get buffeted by animated internal and external stakeholders. Conscious collaboration requires versatility and resilience, together with deep self-awareness—those with strong personal networks and readily accessible social support structures tend to be the ones that thrive and bring energy to the collaboration.

Conscious initiatives are emerging around the world right now and that offers those committed to conscious collaboration an opportunity to connect and share, whether through formal associations, societies or networks such as the RSA,[3] TED[4] or the Do Lectures,[5] or less formal

---

[3] The RSA is the Royal Society for the encouragement of Arts, Manufactures and Commerce—and exists to enrich society through ideas and action. http://www.thersa.org (accessed October 20, 2015).

[4] TED—Technology Entertainment and Ideas—http://www.ted.com (accessed October 20, 2015).

[5] The Do Lectures—http://www.thedolectures.com (accessed October 20, 2015).

networks that use social platforms such as Twitter to link like minds. Books such as Fred Kofman's *Conscious Business*, John Mackey and Raj Sisodia's *Conscious Capitalism*, Otto Scharmer's *Theory U*, Peter Senge's *The Necessary Revolution* and Frédéric Laloux's *Reinventing Organizations* are catalyzing conscious communities that meet to learn and grow.

Where Next?

We know the future is impossibly hard to predict, yet it's possible to see some new ideas and trends emerging. Technology offers us unprecedented opportunities to connect with others around the world and to transform the way we work together, but it doesn't obviate the enduring need for personal integrity and conscious approach to collaboration.

Some thinkers such as Harold Jarche,[6] Lynda Gratton[7] and John Renesch[8] are actively exploring the intersection between consciousness, business, people and organizations, and the future of work, and some of the books mentioned above have covered a range of themes that relate to conscious collaboration, including concepts such as 'wirearchy' and 'holacracy', which they explore in more detail. Our understanding of communities in the workplace is evolving—something my friend Ian Gee and his co-author Matthew Hanwell explore in their book *The Workplace Community*[9]—and this will influence organization design and processes.

Against this backdrop, organizations and their partners will continue to consciously collaborate and learn from each other and the experience. I hope this book and its website catalyzes new thinking about the way we work together, and in time I hope we will be able to consolidate some of the learning and experience and share it much more widely.

For The Conscious Project, we have a role in continuing to work with organizations to help them 'think about what they're doing', and do it better. Developing our nascent virtual guild alongside an exciting

---

[6] http://jarche.com (accessed October 20, 2015).
[7] http://www.lyndagratton.com (accessed October 20, 2015).
[8] http://www.renesch.com (accessed October 20, 2015).
[9] Ian Gee and Matthew Hanwell, *The Workplace Community*, Basingstoke, Palgrave, 2015.

portfolio will keep us occupied for some time yet, but offers a glimpse of a new way of working that creatively connects the social, environmental and financial with purpose and integrity, and is fun!

Final Remarks

And so we come to a few closing remarks. We've been prompted to think deeply about what we seek from our collaboration, and our individual role and contribution. It's clear collaboration isn't the easy option, and it's certainly not for the faint-hearted. It requires flexibility, resilience, tenacity, good humor, humility, generosity, deep self-awareness and much more.

Choosing to work consciously and collaboratively will at times be a messy business. But as I often remind myself when I'm with my young children: 'Making things is messy!' We need to accept that at times conscious collaboration will be scrappy, untidy, messy—and we will stumble through challenges. How—and whether—we pick ourselves up will be crucial, and the way we live the values of conscious collaboration will be what sets the tone for the rest of our partners in collaboration.

It may feel as though it's too late to change the way you're collaborating right now, although I hope that some of the ideas and techniques in this book will be of practical use and will serve to renew your enthusiasm for working as consciously as you possibly can. We owe it to each other to rethink the way we work together, for good. I wish you every success as you choose the path of conscious collaboration, and do keep an eye out for us, we won't be far away!

Index

© The Editor(s) (if applicable) and The Author(s) 2016
B. Emmens, *Conscious Collaboration*,
DOI 10.1057/978-1-137-53805-5